To Jacob

My Best Regards

Your Future in

Health care!

Dave B[illegible]

"I am very happy to see that 'Cash Is King' stresses the mission of hospitals in improving margins. The lifecycle of receivables may be a dry subject to the average reader. However, management of this cycle provides the funds which save lives and keep health care available to everyone.

"Keep up the good work. I believe that you are the best in the field."

Steve Ronstrom
Executive Vice President
St. Francis Medical Center
Monroe, LA

"Well done! Provides the nuts and bolts on the importance of dealing with patient receivables as a part of the overall financial strategy for our hospital. Not just for financial managers but for the CEO as well."

James J. Sexton
President & CEO
St. Agnes Hospital
Fond du Lac, WI

"As with his previous book, 'Turnaround', David Zimmerman has again given hospital executives tremendous insight into the power of cash accumulation strategies. He continues to identify opportunities and supply implementation guidelines for improving cash flow and cash management through accounts receivable in ways that motivate and inspire executive management as well as the staff. As with Mr. Zimmerman's previous publications, 'Cash Is King' is must reading at every level of the organization."

Ronald E. Bartlett
Sr. Vice President for Finance
Newton-Wellesley Hospital
Newton, MA

Cash is KING

OTHER BOOKS BY DAVID ZIMMERMAN

Turnaround Hospital Cash Flow

Winning at Receivables

"It's in the Mail" (co-authored with Bruce Nelson)

Keys to Collecting in Health Care

Keep Peace While Collecting

Twelve Key Strategies to Improving Cash Flow for Medical Groups

Collecting in Health Care

David Zimmerman

Cash is KING

How hospitals can improve the margin to keep the mission.

EAGLE PRESS

Franklin, Wisconsin

Eagle Press
9301 West Rawson
Franklin, Wisconsin 53132

Printed in the United States of America
98 97 96 95 94 93 5 4 3 2 1

ISBN 1-882987-00-4

To Peggy

Contents

Foreword

The current health care situation has to be frustrating for many people. Health care expense now represents over 12 percent of our gross domestic product (GDP) compared to about 5 percent just 10 years ago. Some experts project it will reach 15 percent in a couple of years.

Consumers complain because they are paying an increasing portion of their income for health care. They feel that price increases by hospitals and other providers have gone out of control. Thousands of people in the United States don't even have basic health care available to them, for whatever the reason.

Hospitals complain because their reimbursement for Medicare and Medicaid continues to become a smaller and smaller fraction of their actual cost. They have seen themselves thrust into a very competitive environment, but many are unprepared to manage their costs in a way that other successful businesses have done.

Insurance companies complain because health insurance is no longer a profitable segment for many of them.

Physicians complain because their income is getting squeezed in a managed care setting.

Businesses complain because they have seen more and more of the cost of our health care system shifted to them. Ask any CEO of a mid- to large-sized company what his or her biggest problems are, and the increasing cost of employee health care will probably be first or second on the list.

The end result is a health care delivery system that appears to have serious problems from both a cost and a consumer access viewpoint. In spite of this, many still believe we have the finest medical care available in the world.

This book addresses the deteriorating financial condition of many hospitals. It deals with one of the most important tasks in any enterprise—managing receivables. Its title, *Cash Is King,* gives a clue to the premise of this book: Cash is an absolute necessity for survival. A business can survive, sometimes for several years, without making a profit. But, just as a body dies very quickly if blood flow is stopped, so a business will die quickly if cash flow is stopped.

When I began reading the manuscript of this book for the first time, I kept telling myself, "Just one more chapter, and then I'll go to bed." At 2:00 AM, I finally did put it down, but I had read nearly 25 percent of the entire book. What kept me interested? Two things—the message, and the writing style of its author, David Zimmerman.

The message is quite simple: Many hospitals are going through financial difficulties, including tight cash flow; great improvements will be made if CEOs and CFOs would focus more attention on better management of receivables.

From my perspective as a hospital board member for over 7 years and co-owner of a manufacturing company for 27 years, the importance of cash flow to any successful enterprise cannot be emphasized too strongly. In this book, the author sizes up the situation with plenty of facts and gives specific actions to take. He also relates many success stories of hospitals, showing what they have done and how the resultant increase in cash flow has greatly improved their financial health.

I have known Dave Zimmerman for over 25 years as a personal friend. When I first met him, he was the business manager of a not-for-profit hospital. Over the ensuing years, he continued his career path in the health care industry with positions in HFMA, Blue Cross, and finally, as a consultant to hospitals. As he became more exposed to worsening financial conditions in hospitals, he became convinced that part of the problem was that cursory attention was being given to managing receivables in many of them. It was with this background that the seeds were planted for what was to become his mission: To show hospitals how to manage their receivables in a much better way in order to free up cash and prevent financial crises.

Dave is very passionate about this mission. Anyone who has ever heard him give a seminar or worked with him in a hospital project will know what I mean. He believes strongly that a great deal of the financial trouble that hospitals are experiencing today would have been avoided by a diligent effort to better manage their receivables.

I suggest that anyone, especially hospital CEOs and CFOs, having an interest or concern in the financial condition of any hospital will profit much from reading this book. You will find it easy to read, very informative, and hopefully, it will move you to take action.

ROBERT A. GUNDERSON
Vice Chairman, Board of Directors
St. Francis Hospital
Milwaukee, Wisconsin

Preface

Clinton's victory could be hospitals' loss

Now that Bill Clinton has been elected President, what will be the impact in hospital cash and profit? My advice, buckle up!

Major health reform was a major topic of Clinton's since early in his campaign. Controlling rising health spending has been number one on his agenda in the reform message. In fact, he's promised to have a reform plan to the Congress in his first 100 days in office.

His appointment of Judith Feder, a proponent of health care overhaul, as his administration's health policy director, shows that he means to consider major changes in the system. Controlling your charges will be at the top of the list.

What we don't know as this book goes to press, is just what form his total reform package will take. Clinton said he would deal with the 35 million uninsured Americans by implementing a "play-or-pay" reform plan that would require American employers to either buy insurance for their workers or pay a payroll tax to the government, which would cover the uninsured in a public program.

As time wore on, this plan was extremely unpopular, so Clinton began to separate himself from play-or-pay and in late September, scraped it altogether.

Having dumped play-or-pay, Clinton has trouble explaining what his new plan is. Clinton says he would require employers to insure their workers either directly or by buying coverage from a purchasing group. For the nonworking uninsured, Clinton says he would "guarantee private coverage...starting with pregnant women and children." And he would pay for coverage of that group with savings achieved in government health programs as a result of cost containment.

While Clinton is flip-flopping about what he will do for the uninsured, he's been very clear about what he wants to do about the cost control issue in health care. He proposes a system of national budgeting for health spending that will cap inflation. He also wants to streamline paperwork to cut administrative costs.

His global budget would be set up by a board of consumers, providers and business leaders to decide how much the country could spend on providing health care for everyone.

If Clinton is successful in getting this national board in place quickly and gets a national budget in place in the first year of his presidency, you could see some serious budgeting going on in your hospital. Improving cash will be even more important for hospitals than it is today.

If an inflationary cap is in place by fiscal year '94, the profit and cash flow at your hospital could take a hit. Our suggestion is you start doing something now to improve employee performance and increase cash collected as a percent of your net revenue. This book has plenty of tips to help you make that happen.

Clinton's victory could be your hospital's loss. Time will tell.

DAVE ZIMMERMAN

Acknowledgments

Several people helped to put *Cash Is King* together. Steve Chrapla, Pattie Kloehn, Chuck Lund and Bruce Nelson provided valuable research while Patti Landreman typed the first draft from my barely legible hand written notes.

Laura Merisalo and Heather Haschka did the proofreading and Kathi Isaacson Hamm typeset and laid out the entire book. The book jacket was designed by Ed Musial.

And finally, my wife, Peg, gave me the original idea for the book.

1

Cash Is King

**Cash flow—not profitability—
is truest indication of a hospital's
financial viability**

HEALTH CARE IS BIG BUSINESS

Make no mistake about it. Health care is a business today. A very big business.

Although propelled by the noblest of missions, health care has become a huge industry—one of the largest and most volatile in the nation.

Total health care expenditures came in over $800 billion in 1992. Hospitals alone created over $300 billion of that figure.[1]

Health care expenditures accounted for less than 5 percent of the nation's gross national product back in 1950. It will consume 14 percent of the GNP in 1992, and is projected

[1] Source: U.S. Department of Commerce

to be as much as 40 percent of the GNP by the year 2030. President Clinton has said health care spending will get priority attention by his administration.

Amazingly, while all this money is exchanging hands between payers and providers of health care, most hospitals are cash poor. While operating profits have begun to show some improvement, many are still short of cash. Reserves are down. As a result, investment income has suffered in recent years and with Clinton's plan to cap charges, cash will be even tighter in the next four years.

The single most critical financial problem facing many hospitals today is cash flow.

Chief financial and chief executive officers time and again complain, "If I'm making a profit, why don't we have any money?"

A hospital can't pay bills and employee salaries with profits, only cash.

While lack of available cash becomes a critical issue for many hospitals, it also has a damaging rippling affect. A larger number of hospitals are getting turned away from tax-exempt bond investors.

Many hospitals desperately need cash to renovate, start long overdue construction, buy equipment or refinance debt. Delays in much needed capital can bury some hospitals.

In some cases, inability to gain access to the capital market may be one more factor that forces a hospital to close, or just limp along getting more antiquated and outdated each year.

According to one study, 19 percent of all hospitals were considered to be in financial distress in mid-1992. Health Care Investment Analysts, a Baltimore-based health care research firm that compiles the quarterly study, expects the level of troubled hospitals to remain constant or increase slightly.

During the last decade, hospitals have fought the battle of trying to increase revenue while expenses escalate. For too many, it's a losing battle.

The reality is most hospitals simply do not have enough cash.

CASH IS KING

Cash is king. Even the noblest of missions cannot survive without it.

Cash flow—not profitability—is the truest indication of a hospital's financial viability. Cash flow statements report on a hospital's investing and financial activities—its cash inflow and outflows over a period of time. By contrast, balance sheets provide only a "snapshot" of the status of assets, liabilities and equities at the end of that period.

Traditionally, hospitals compare and report their financial statistics to each other. Comparisons always are to other hospitals—by comparable bed size, location, etc.

Recent cash flow variable comparisons show hospital net days revenue outstanding in the mid-70s and payables averaging a 38-day turnaround.[2] It doesn't take an economist to see that is an unhealthy combination. Money from receivables is coming in considerably slower than it is going out to pay bills, contributing to the cash poor situation.

The result of a poor days revenue outstanding to payable days is reflected in hospitals' days cash on hand statistic.

Days cash on hand, a measure of a hospital's liquidity, for all hospitals was an alarmingly low 24 days early in 1992.[3] For hospitals over 50 beds, the average dropped to an even lower 21 days cash on hand.

---

[2] American Hospital Association Monitrend, first quarter 1992.

[3] Hospital Administrative Services Monitrend

Not a healthy situation.

Comparing financial statistics among themselves is one thing, but should hospitals compare their financial performance with other industries? Or is there just no sense in comparing hospitals to any other kind of business?

Bill Cleverley, Ph.D., CPA, Professor of Hospital and Health Administration at Ohio State University, Columbus, has compared non-profit hospitals to a variety of industries in several key financial performances. The comparisons in profitability, liquidity, financial risk, asset management and net days outstanding show hospitals woefully on the short end of the stick.

Cleverley and Roger Harvey, a professor of finance at Ohio State, co-authored a report that pointed out not-for-profit hospitals exhibit serious weaknesses in several areas. They didn't pull any punches in laying out the comparisons and stating that most hospitals are in more trouble than they realize.

HOSPITALS IN TROUBLE

Because hospitals have traditionally measured their financial performance against themselves, and as the numbers grew gradually worse for all the nation's hospitals, the comparisons didn't show how bad off hospitals really were. Cleverley's analysis hits home like a ton of bricks.

These comparisons point out hospitals should aim toward higher operating margins, strive for a better return on equity and improve net days revenue outstanding. These comparisons may serve as a wake-up call for hospitals' senior executives. Hospitals are worse off financially than many people think.

Another telling statistic that impacts available cash for hospitals is the huge amount of contractual allowances that have eaten into profits at an alarming rate in recent years.

By mid-year in 1992, hospitals were averaging nearly 35 percent of their revenue in contractual allowances.

The "funny money" floating through hospital financial statements is no longer a joke. Rather, what started out as an amusing little allowance in Medicare reimbursement in 1966, has become a pitiful, bad joke for hospitals.

Now, all health care payers are joining the frolic and creating massive allowances to hospital charges that threaten to turn the entire reimbursement process into the ridiculous.

"Funny money," or contractual allowances from Medicare, Medicaid, managed care and the Blues, constitute nearly 35 percent of hospitals' total revenue, according to Monitrend, American Hospital Association. As a result, hospital CFOs shuffle the cost and opportunity to make a profit over to the remaining commercial carriers and patients. This facetious play on words is not raising any laughter in hospital board rooms these days.

"Cost shifting" to make a profit by hospitals from private payers is driven by Medicare and Medicaid payment shortfalls, according to Allen Dobson, Ph.D., of the Lewin-ICF health care policy and institutional consulting firm, based in Washington, D.C.

In 1989, Dobson reports, the estimated level of undercompensated care from public payers, $11.2 billion, was reasonably close to the $8.9 billion cost of unsponsored care provided to patients in the form of bad debt and charity care. By 1992, however, undercompensated care from public payers will total $22.7 billion, nearly twice the $11.9 billion cost to hospitals of totally uncompensated care.

MEDICARE PAYMENTS CAUSE CASH CRUNCH

Every time a hospital admits a Medicare patient in 1993 it will lose about $900, according to the latest AHA projections. Those projections show that, overall, Medicare payments will fall $9 billion short of what hospitals will spend caring for Medicare inpatients during fiscal year 1993.

In addition, the AHA projected that the national aggregate Prospective Payment System margin for FY 1993 will be negative 15 percent, or 3.2 percent below that for FY 1992. If the AHA's projections hold true, more than 70 percent of hospitals will report negative PPS margins for FY 1993, and those with beds between 100 to 299 will be hardest hit.

Cost shifting has grown from $20.1 billion to $34.6 billion between 1989 and 1992, the Lewin-ICF report notes. This may produce a major destabilizing effect on the financing of health care services as various "stakeholders," such as employers, government, and hospitals, react in different ways.

Although employers currently fund the cost shift, "the business community eventually will reject cost shifting as an implicit societal policy for financing indigent health care and governmental underpayment," according to the report. Hospitals bear the brunt of the cost shift, serving as "quasi-governmental bodies, imposing taxes on one set of patients to cover the unreimbursed cost of another," Lewin-ICF reports.

To the extent hospitals cannot reduce costs to the level of Medicare/Medicaid payments, the report states, the industry "will deteriorate physically and financially. Access to care and quality of care could be adversely affected."

Recent studies show that employers view HMOs, PPOs and other forms of managed care with mixed results. In general, most companies are not crazy about their small savings shown through managed care. It varies by plan and part of the country, but the trend of smaller savings are there.

Hospitals are beginning to have those same disappointments in their managed care contracts. Studies show that while managed care contracts may help fill beds (at least for a while), too many hospitals can't make any money on their managed care contracts.

In fact, some hospitals are taking a financial beating in managed care. If managed care continues to increase, as most health care financial experts predict, hospitals around the nation may feel the financial pinch.

COST SHIFTING COMING TO AN END

Cost shifting is coming to an end. It will mark the end of an era. With the continuous spread of managed care into reimbursement, there will be nowhere to shift—except to the patient, and that has been curtailed with President Clinton's plan for a health care spending cap.

In my opinion, hospitals have less than four years to turn around their financial performance before the government takes on more control of health care spending and reimbursement. It will take better management to offset the inevitable financial loss. Senior hospital executives desperately need to figure out ways to generate more cash.

Because cash is king in this health care business—just as it is in all others, generating more cash for hospitals is what this book is all about.

In my opinion, hospitals now rely too heavily on over-sold advertising and internal cost-cutting to improve the bottom line and create more cash. What the industry is overlooking, is the vast potential of improving cash flow and profit with better management of receivables and the reduction of bad debt.

Current estimates show that hospitals will write off nearly $14 billion in bad debt in 1993.[4] That figure will continue to skyrocket if allowed to run at its current pace because of increasing deductibles and co-payments.

I would predict an entirely different scenario if hospital senior executives would maximize the untapped potential of accounts receivable. The projected $14 billion in bad debt for 1993 alone could be slashed in half if hospitals would refocus their financial efforts.

I also would say unequivocally, that hospitals' average net days, which for the past several years have hovered in the mid-70s, should be in the mid-50s. That shift alone would improve cash flow $4.6 billion and generate $300 million a year in investment income.

Receivables long have been undervalued as an excellent opportunity to improve cash flow and profit. This book will attempt to change that.

[4] Zimmerman & Associates, Inc., *HARA (Hospital Accounts Receivable Analysis)*, 1992.

2

No Margin—No Mission

If the hospital can't generate enough cash or make enough profit to grow, the mission it has identified for itself cannot be carried out.

MISSION DEPENDS ON MARGIN OF PROFIT

No margin, no mission. Simple, but true.

If the hospital can't generate enough cash or make enough profit to stay alive or grow, the mission it has identified for itself cannot be carried out. However, I think CEOs have a dilemma with this money-mission thing. A recent study by Professional Research Consultants, based on the responses from 250 hospital CEOs, shows mission overrides money by those CEOs.

Every voluntary hospital CEO faces the daily pressure of running the hospital like a "charitable" organization while performing like a business. But when dealing with such situations, more than 65 percent of CEOs recently surveyed by

Hospitals say they tip the balance heavily in favor of mission. Money was a far distant second at 19 percent.

CEOs say "mission" takes precedence over "margin".

Question: "In general, which pursuit is more important for a hospital's success?"

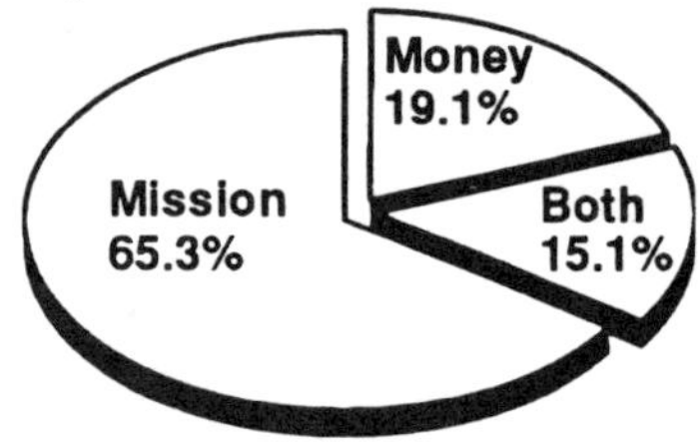

Source: *Hospitals* magazine

On the other hand, hospital CEOs and CFOs realize if their hospital's financial situation deteriorates, mission will go down the tubes along with the hospital. In short, if there is no margin—forget the mission.

In my 30 years in health care, it has always been so—mission over money for hospitals. Not so anymore.

Today, CEOs need to pay more attention to how their hospital is going to become more profitable. In fact, financial performance should be uppermost in CEOs minds these days. Their survival is tied to how well the hospital does financially. Right in the middle of recent controversy over hospital CEO high compensation levels, a survey conducted by the Hay Group revealed that, for the most part, executive pay levels in health care are linked to financial performance.

Hospital CEOs who get fired are more likely to be evaluated based on financial performance than on the CEOs' relationships with their board, or their integrity or judgment. If they couldn't produce a good bottom line, nothing could save them.

To understand the causes of executive turnover, a study was conducted by the American College of Healthcare Executives, the American Hospital Association, and Heidrick & Struggles Inc. The study by the three Chicago-based organizations, revealed several characteristics of high turnover hospitals—facilities with more than two CEO turnovers.

Criteria used in recent CEO evaluation

Criteria considered	Rank of importance in evaluation
Economic performance of hospital	1
Medical staff relations	2
Quality of care	3
Long-range strategies	4
Short-term operational plans	5
Personal qualities	6
Compliance with regulations and accreditation standards	7
Crisis prevention	8
Malpractice liability control	9
Other	10

Source: The American Hospital Association Data Center, Chicago

I'm very familiar with and fully supportive of a hospital's mission, having spent 17 years as an employee at two different hospitals. However, while "mission" still is the major reason hospitals exist, without sound financial footing, no amount of noble intentions will hold a hospital together in today's marketplace.

I CAN RELATE TO MISSION

Hospital mission and a high quality of medical care makes me think back to a few years ago and our daughter, Janie. About a month after our seventh child was born, Peggy and I learned Jane would need open heart surgery. The doctors explained Jane had two holes in her heart—called an atrium septal and ventricle septal defect. We were shocked. Now what? Yes, she was to need open heart surgery to repair the defects. No, they didn't want to do it yet. Go home, take care of her, love her a lot, and wait.

We didn't have long to wait. Within weeks, she had heart failure, then pneumonia. Back to the hospital. Then home again and back again. This went on for almost two months. Although Jane was putting up a courageous fight, she was losing ground.

Then, suddenly, she began to recover from the pneumonia and her vital signs improved enough for the doctor to consider the surgery. He explained that the operation only had a 50-50 chance of success.

The surgical team described the eight-hour process to us. A technician carefully diagrammed how the equipment would be used in the operation and answered all of our questions. Even though I had spent almost my entire professional career in or around hospitals, I was amazed at the technology. I was struck by the progress made in recent years in open heart surgery on young children.

Thanks to an excellent surgeon, his fine team and a dedicated staff at Children's Hospital of Wisconsin, Jane pulled through the operation with flying colors. Today, just more than five years after her open heart surgery, she is healthy, active and, I must admit, terribly spoiled. But, somewhere during the time we were sitting nervously in the waiting room on that overcast, snowy, winter day of her surgery, it hit me.

Suddenly, it became clear to me that this country has the finest medical care available to more people than anywhere in the world—That lives like Jane's are being saved every minute in hospitals throughout the nation.

It's clear that sick and injured people are being made whole again in hospitals around the nation. And, that their tremendously advanced medical care takes cash to continue—lots of cash. And, that the people primarily responsible for providing the financial security of this industry were the key executives of hospitals—the CEOs, COOs, CFOs and yes—the managers in charge of the receivables. It was their job—maybe mine, and other consultants like me—to be sure our quality of health care didn't regress.

Practically every day we read of another "medical miracle" just like our Janie's. For instance, in 1991 one-year survival rates achieved by 91 percent of the nation's 531 hospital-based organ-transplant programs met or exceeded expected survival rates, according to a government study.

MEDICAL MISSIONS TAKE MONEY

Tell me, who in their right mind wants anything to happen that will slow medical research and progress? This medical progress takes money, and lots of it. Proper management of hospitals' largest asset, receivables, will go some distance toward ensuring that nothing will happen to this kind of progress. Hospitals will, indeed, keep their mission alive through sound receivables management.

Keeping hospitals open and vibrant is a part of all of our responsibility.

Since 1980, over 600 acute-care hospitals have closed their doors. Low occupancy and financial difficulties have been given as the major reasons for these facilities failing. Although according to the American Hospital Association, 1992 has seen fewer closings than in prior years, there is still a lot to be concerned about in our industry.

Health Care Investment Analysts Inc., of Baltimore, has published median values of indicators for, as they call them, *distressed hospitals.*

Median values for HCIA's *Distressed Hospitals*

	1990
Occupancy rate	43%
Days in accounts receivable	**79**
Days cash on hand	**8**
Debt service coverage ratio	0.47
Operating margin	-7.81%
Total profit margin	-6.49%

Will the nations' hospitals' financial situation improve much in the next few years? No. In fact, it will get worse, according to a group of 28 health care financial experts.

The Healthcare Financial Management Association recently put a panel of experienced hospital finance people together. Their objective was to look out a few years and paint a picture of the future. What they saw was bleak.

Unfortunately, they foresee continued declines in financial performance all the way through 1995. The panel predicted hospitals will begin to feel even more of a financial pinch as they continuously lose their ability to cost shift to make up the losses from Medicare and Medicaid contractual allowance write-offs.

Overall, they see operating margins slipping further by 1995.

The panel sees no improvement in accounts receivable for hospitals over the next three years. They feel days revenue outstanding will remain in the mid-70s, as it is today. They see bad debt and charity increasing between now and 1995.

Fortunately, predictions of this nature can be altered. They can be altered by hospital CEOs and CFOs who are success and results oriented. These gloomy forecasts of mundane mediocrity do not have to materialize. Individually and collectively, hospitals can reverse these projections.

RECEIVABLES MAY MAKE THE DIFFERENCE

How receivables are managed the next few years may be the heart of the difference. Executives who make it one of their major goals to improve their receivables will do so. We've seen many recent examples where hospitals flew into the face of adversity and brought their days outstanding under 60 and bad debt well under two percent.

Well-managed receivables will go a long way toward reversing these premature predictions.

There is no question in my mind that net days revenue outstanding can average in the mid-50s for most of the nation's hospitals. I'd also bet the house that the majority of hospitals could cut their bad debt in half with improved management of their receivables.

However, hospital executives have to ask themselves, "Are we managing receivables the way we think we *could* be? Are we getting the results that we think we *should* be?"

Recently, I talked to a young man who said he became director of receivables at a hospital a couple of years ago, when they were losing $20 million a year. Then, there was a change in management. A lot of new people came in.

Now, the hospital is only $1 million in the red. In a relatively short period of time, the hospital has gone from a $20 million to a $1 million annual loss, and a big improvement in receivables was a major reason.

I see numerous examples almost every month graphically displaying how hospitals are having a tough time making a buck in operations today. One of the reasons is that days outstanding are far too high. Days outstanding average about

75 to 80 in the hospital industry. Other industry figures average closer to 45. Any time most other industries exceed 45 days in cash flow turnaround of days revenue outstanding, it spells trouble—serious trouble.

One of the reasons we are having trouble in our industry is because our turnaround of receivables is too slow. Hospital receivables are not well managed in most hospitals. Despite an increase in automation, the picture hasn't changed much in the past three or four years. We have been in the mid-70s now for three or four years. It's simply too high.

BE CONVINCED: RECEIVABLES NEED TO IMPROVE

People come to my seminars and say, "I want some answers." My thinking is, first of all I have to convince you there is some room for improvement. My experience has been, until you are convinced that you can improve, not much happens.

In a number of cases (and you probably have seen this, too), people are given the "to-do" list. All you have to do is go back to your shop and "do it." How many seminars have you been to in your life? Many, no doubt.

In every one of those programs, they give you a list of things that you can do. You hurry back and you do it, right? Sure! Most of us take this stuff, we put it into our desk drawer, and we find it the next time we move offices.

Then you say, "I had a good time attending that seminar, and I have all these good notes that I forgot I had taken."

Sometimes we get so busy after coming back from these seminars that what happens? We never have time to put into effect good ideas we have learned. Part of the reason is this—there was no strong desire to take this information and put it to use. Most of the time, you have the information, but now it is a matter of *wanting* to use it.

It is a shame that most of us get so caught up in our day-to-day activities that we forget sometimes *why* we are there. We forget what we are doing is serving patients. We forget the noble profession that we are in, and why we should be successful, the *real* reason for being successful. We forget the mission.

You see, it is my contention that when you are thoroughly convinced, as are many of the hospital managers across the United States, that what you are doing is extremely important, then you will have a higher dedication and commitment to excellence.

Let's face it, the only one who can really address the issue of cash the quickest is the health care industry itself—certainly not the government, not insurance companies and not the public. It's going to come down to people who hold responsible positions within the health care providers' organizations to make the big difference.

Improvement in revenue turnaround time and cutting bad debt is a sure way for the nation's hospitals to play a major role in impacting hospital finances and, perhaps more importantly, actually having the opportunity to change the course of history in this industry. What you do to improve cash and profit in the next few years may very well dictate what happens to this industry in the decades to come.

3

Unleash the Potential

Hospital receivables have great potential for improving profits and cash. It's the industry's best-kept secret. Faster turnover of receivables and reduction in bad debt would pump billions back into the system.

RECEIVABLES OFFER OUTSTANDING POTENTIAL

Do you think we are exaggerating the importance of receivables on cash and profit? What impact would faster turnover of receivables and a reduction in bad debt have on the nation's hospitals' financial condition?

Probably billions. "Mega" dollars could be pumped back into the system. Take a look at these numbers.

Calculation of potential cost benefits for hospital industry

End of 1992:
Total national A/R net dollars
outstanding .... $17.1 billion

Targeted cash flow improvement
(to 55 net days) .... $4.6 billion

Projected investment income:
(based on 6 percent) .... Over $275 million annually

Estimated 1993 write-off to bad debt .... $14 billion

Targeted 50% improvement to 2.75% .... $7 billion

First year impact of improved receivables management in hospitals

Cash flow improvement to 55 net days .... $4.6 billion

Investment income at 6% .... $275 million

Reduction of bad debt to 2.75% .... $7 billion

Total potential first year .... $11.6 billion[1]

If hospitals turned their receivables around in an average of 55 (net) days, it would put nearly $5 billion into hospitals! If the bad debt was reduced by half—the net result would put another $7 billion back into hospitals. And these are annual figures. Who says better management of the receivables couldn't have a major impact? How about those figures for motivation?

Take your own hospital for instance. What kind of dollars would you put back into your system if you were at 55 days (net) and your bad debt was half of what it is now?

Because your hospital actually "sells on credit," you have an investment in accounts receivable—it's a fact of business life.

HIDDEN PROFITS

Less obvious is the net effect this sizable investment can have on your earnings, over and above the normal costs associated

[1] Zimmerman & Associates, Inc., *HARA (Hospital Accounts Receivable Analysis)*, 4th Quarter, 1992.

with the credit and collection effort. Indeed, you may find reducing your investment in accounts receivable uncovers thousands of dollars in "hidden" profits.

Net days outstanding over 60 days for most hospitals is strong evidence of some fundamental management problem—perhaps weak management, poor policies, poor collection efforts, lack of focus, or whatever. What is important here, however, is the effect the longer collection period has on your hospital's investment in accounts receivable, and, in turn, the detrimental effect that investment has on earnings.

The cost of carrying accounts receivable

Average collection period (net days)	Average accounts receivable	Annual cost 10%
30	$3 million	$300,000
35	$3.5 million	$300,500
40	$4 million	$400,000
50	$5 million	$500,000
60	$6 million	$600,000

The lower investment in accounts receivable—and consequent reduction in interest costs—can lead to a respectable increase in earnings.

Don't underestimate the profit potential that may be hidden in your accounts receivable. The profit doesn't come directly from the receivables, but from the reduced costs of carrying a smaller investment.

Use the chart above to apply this concept to your hospital. It illustrates the effect the average collection period has on a hospital's investment in accounts receivable, as well as the cost of carrying that investment.

Referring to the chart, if your hospital generates $100,000 per day in net revenue, a 45-day collection period results in a $4.5 million investment in accounts receivable. Moreover, assuming a 10 percent annual rate, you incur a $450,000 expense to carry that investment. Your specific carrying cost should be measured by your own borrowing cost.

Now, consider the bottom-line benefits you gain from even a modest reduction in average collection period. A five-day reduction reduces your investment in accounts receivable by $500,000, and the expense of carrying that investment by $50,000. The larger your revenue, the larger the bottom-line benefits you realize from a comparable reduction in collection period.

Certainly, you should make your assessment in light of other factors. Perhaps your investment in receivables is appropriate for your net revenue. Or, you may find the cost of reducing your average collection period greater than the return. But not likely. Improved management of your receivables frequently can accelerate collections and lead to immediate bottom-line benefits.

Finally, don't disregard the hidden profit potential in your receivables because you are debt-free. The hospital that doesn't borrow still incurs a cost when it carries accounts receivable. It isn't a direct cost, but an indirect or "opportunity cost"—the loss of potential earnings from funds tied up in an overinvestment in receivables. Freeing those funds allows you to increase profits by expanding inventory, taking purchasing discounts, or investing the funds and earning interest.

Indeed, the cost of carrying your accounts receivable may not always be obvious—but it is always real. Recognize that cost and you may uncover hundreds of thousands of dollars in hidden profits.

IMPROVEMENTS LEAD TO ADDITIONAL CASH

Hospitals making improvements by reducing their days revenue outstanding and bad debt can add up to some big dollars. For instance, a typical 120-bed hospital with 77 days outstanding and 5 percent bad debt could improve their cash flow by $760,000 and annual profit potential by $395,000 with a 10-day reduction in days outstanding and a decrease in bad debt to 3 percent.

Calculation of potential cost benefits

A. 10-day improvement in gross days revenue outstanding	
1. Gross revenue (12-month period)	$22.2 million
a. Days in period	365
b. Average daily gross revenue	$61,000
c. Allowance for net revenue	70%
2. Average daily net revenue	$42,700
3. Targeted improvement GDRO	10 days
4. Estimated cash flow improvement	$427,000
5. Projected cost of funds (investment growth)	8%
6. Potential increased yield on the $427,000 (investment income)	$34,160
B. Reduction in uncollectibles to 3.5% from 5%	
1. Total uncollectibles (12-month period)	$1.1 million
2. Proposed reduction	30%
3. Estimated cash flow improvement and profit improvement	$334,000
4. Projected cost of funds	8%
5. Potential increased yield on the $334,000 (investment income)	$26,718
C. Summary of profit potential	
1. 10-day improvement in GDRO	$427,000
2. Increased investment yield	$34,160
3. 30% reduction in uncollectibles	$334,000
4. Uncollectible investment yield	$26,718
5. Total (not including 10-day cash flow improvement)	$395,000

Here's how the computation might look in this example:

This current asset of receivables is most valuable when quickly converted to cash. It doesn't do any good sitting in receivables or being written off to bad debt. With net days revenue outstanding nationally at the mid-70s, millions of dollars could be collected faster. And the bad debt bleeding must be stopped. In fact, it's gone beyond bleeding; now, it's hemorrhaging.

Our national survey of hospitals, *HARA (Hospital Accounts Receivable Analysis),* indicated hospitals spend an average of 2.4

cents to collect every dollar in their receivables.

I believe this low ratio of expense-to-collect is one reason why the days in receivables are as high as they are. It is no coincidence hospitals operating with gross days outstanding under 60 days are spending more in the management of their receivables.

This dilemma comes down to "pay now or pay later". You either invest in managing better internally or pay the price in slow turnaround of cash and heavy write-offs along with higher collection agency costs.

When receivables *are not* collected, cash may not be available to meet operating expenses. This may result in added interest expense for operating loans. With the prime rate at 8.5 percent, you would be paying a lot more than the current 2.4 percent presently being spent by hospitals for collections.

When receivables *are* collected, cash is available for investment. The absence of investment income can put additional pressure on your income statement.

Accounts receivable not collected will eventually hit your bottom line as a bad debt expense. Uncollectible write-offs were reported at 6 percent of the total gross patient revenue in the second quarter of last year, and the dollars have been increasing over the past 10 years.

COST SHIFTING BITING THE HAND THAT FEEDS IT

Adding to the challenge of managing receivables more profitably is the black hole of cost shifting. The dilemma of cost shifting is starting to bite the hand that feeds it. As time goes on, it looks more and more like the shift will just shimmy and shake the cost on down to the patient. As a result, higher bad debt. Because Medicare, Medicaid, HMOs and PPOs steadily cut back on payments, hospitals continue to shift the cost to catch up on to the other payers to try to make a profit.

In this process, the commercial insurance companies and patients now are bearing the brunt of the cost shift. However, large employers and those firms who are self-insured sidestep much of this cost shifting. They hold the upper hand by driving a hard bargain with hospitals for more contractual allowances. They dodge most of the cost shift and strip hospitals of profit potential.

So, as a result, this cost shifting hits the smaller employer (with a large percent of the employed work force in the United States) right between the eyes.

Small employers, by nature of their size, lack leverage in the health care market. They are unable to evade the cost shift by entering into negotiated care contracts. Therefore, they are compelled to purchase indemnity policies and accept lofty premium increases. Worse, they can be forced to abandon their coverage, thus producing more uninsured patients and

Cost shifting as a percentage of hospital bills

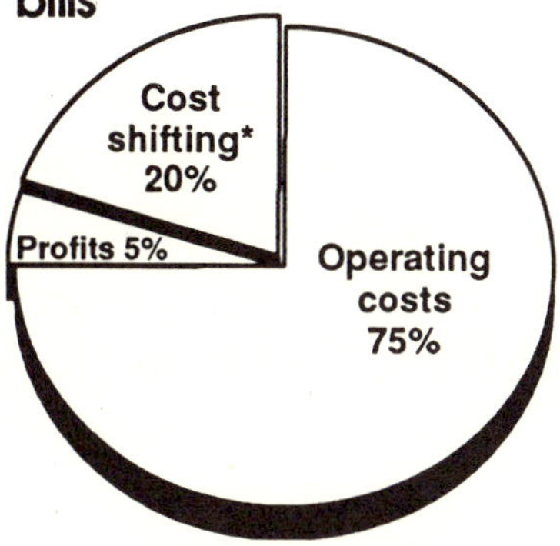

* From unsponsored care and government payment shortfalls to private payers.

Source: American Hospital Association, Chicago

Payment as a percentage of hospitals' costs

Hospitals get less than they spend for many patients.

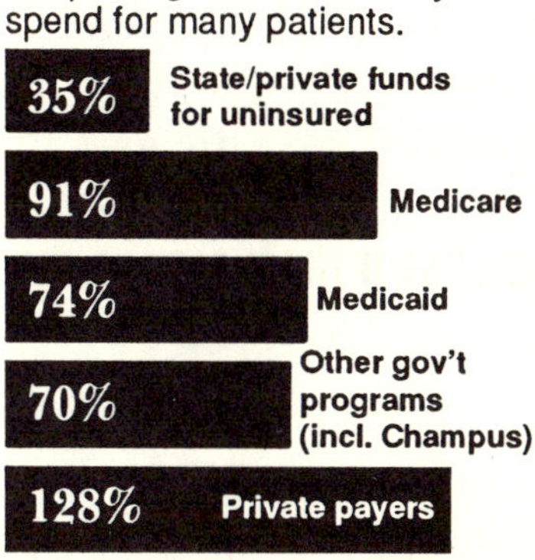

Source: Prospective Payment Assessment Commission, Washington

higher bad debt and charity.

POTENTIAL FADES WITH BAD DEBT

Too much profit potential escapes hospitals in the form of bad debt. Poor collection effectiveness can cripple a hospital. Unfortunately, ineffective collection usually is disguised under the heading of "uncompensated care."

During the 1980s, uncompensated care costs, defined as bad debts and charity care, increased 12 percent per year for acute care hospitals that treat Medicare patients. By 1989, those costs reached over $10 billion, according to a recent Prospective Payment Assessment Commission (ProPAC) report.

This year, based on our survey numbers, we are estimating the nation's hospital bad debt and charity will actually climb to over $20 billion! Hospital bad debt and charity reported in *HARA (Hospital Accounts Receivable Analysis)* averaged 6 percent in 1992. If that average holds up in 1993, the total write-off would reach $20 billion-plus. According to the ProPAC report, urban and rural hospitals shared the burden of *uncompensated* care almost equally in the 1980s.

By collecting more of your self-pay and writing off less to bad debt, your profits can increase substantially. Here's a case-in-point: The nation's community hospitals earned $7 billion in profits in calendar year 1990, according to new financial data released recently by a congressional advisory panel. During that same year, hospitals wrote off $11 billion[2] to bad debt.

Another look: $7 billion profit; $11 billion bad debt. Not a healthy ratio. You can add another $5 billion write-off to charity for 1990, for a total write-off to uncollectibles of $16

[2] Source: Zimmerman & Associates, Inc., *HARA (Hospital Accounts Receivable Analysis)*, Fourth Quarter 1990

billion. Hospitals wrote off 4 percent of their charges to bad debt and two percent to charity in 1990.

Look at the impact of improving collection of your receivables. If the nation's hospitals could have reduced their bad debt write-off by one-half, their profits would have been closer to $12 billion. As a result, hospitals also could have curtailed the increase in charges and taken off some of the heat for runaway expenses. The more hospitals can collect and the less they write off to bad debt, the less they need to increase charges and shift costs to commercial carriers and patients.

More evidence has been uncovered to prove that well-managed receivables can make a big difference in a hospital's overall financial success.

A study recently released by the Healthcare Financial Management Association showed that those hospitals doing better financially also consistently do better in the collection of accounts receivable, carrying five days less in 1990 than low performance hospitals.

HFMA defined high performance and low performance hospitals using a return on investment ratio that removes the effects of inflation. Hospitals with a return on investment of less than 7 percent fell into the low performance group, while those with a ratio greater than 12 percent were considered high performers.

Major HFMA findings include:

- Operating margins have improved for high performance hospitals, which earned 6.2 percent in 1990, compared to minus 1.7 percent for low performance hospitals.
- Liquidity, which measures an organization's ability to fund financial needs, also varies between high and low performance hospitals. The days cash-on-hand ratio, a measure of liquidity, was 21.6 for high performance hospitals and 15.2

for low performance hospitals.

HFMA's analysis is based on audited financial statements from more than 1,300 hospitals included in the association's Financial Analysis Service database over a five-year period.

The strong get stronger and the weak get weaker—in hospital finances. For instance, hospitals with strong financial numbers can climb into the rare stratosphere of being practically debt-free, flush with cash and can choose to fund replacement and meet equipment needs with minimal debt.

A recent article in *Modern Healthcare* profiled one of those hospitals—Children's Hospital of Philadelphia. The author, Judith Nemes, explains how the hospital recently embarked on a $202 million debt financing project, with the intention of capitalizing on its financial muscle and historically low debt.

Their financial strength has given them the wherewithal to get low interest rates at a time when they are planning major projects. Nemes noted that before a recent financing, Children's Hospital had $48 million in outstanding debt. The facility's debt-to-capitalization ratio was 18 percent, much less than the 41.5 percent median for hospitals rated Aa by Moody's Investors Service. Children's Hospital has an Aa rating from Moody's and an AA rating from Standard & Poor's Corp.

In the article, Standard & Poor's said the hospital has posted strong operating and profit margins, averaging 4 percent and 13 percent, respectively, for the past five years. In 1990, children's hospitals nationwide reported average operating margins of 1.1 percent, said the National Association of Children's Hospitals and Related Institutions, Alexandria, Va.

Children's Hospital of Philadelphia reported net income of $29.4 million on net patient revenues of $166 million in 1991, according to audited financial statements. The facility projects it will post net income of $41.4 million on net patient revenues of $189.5 million in 1992.

IMPACTS RESERVES, INVESTMENT INCOME AND RATING

As a result of this kind of financial brawn, Children's Hospital is one of the few hospitals in the nation that have earned a well-deserved Aa rating from Moody's. Only 6 percent of the 700 unenhanced hospitals reviewed by the agency have this high rating.

As a result of this Aa rating, the cost of capital decreases substantially for hospitals, which translates into substantial savings.

Modern Healthcare pointed out in their article that the savings were significant for Children's Hospital in its recent borrowing. They sold $127 million in long-term debt without credit enhancement, and locked in an average interest rate of 6.76%.

Modern Healthcare pointed out by comparison, a BBB-rated hospital issuing the same amount of debt last month would have had to pay nearly $1 million in additional interest per year over the life of the bonds, according to Thomas D. Whalen, a vice president at Smith Barney, Harris Upham & Co., a New York investment firm that acted as lead manager on the hospital's recent bond sale.

Hospitals that keep their days outstanding in the 50s and a low bad debt, will find it a good deal easier to build their reserves, increase investment income and get closer to the better credit ratings and lower interest on short term loans.

If you read this far and are wondering what CEOs or CFOs can do to maximize the potential from receivables, without running down to the business office and managing it themselves, perhaps you'll be intrigued enough to read on.

Relax—this is not a how-to book on managing receivables. I've written enough of those already. Your receivables manager and business office staff should read those.

What we hope to accomplish in this book is to convince senior executives that they have a critical role to play in maximizing this potential, and that if they push the right buttons, cash can be improved dramatically. Our intention is that it is not necessarily doing more things, but the right things right.

In the following chapters, we'll attempt to point out the major hot buttons hospital CEOs and CFOs can push to maximize the potential from their receivables.

It is possible you will feel this book less important for what it says than for what it makes you think.

4

The Quick Fix Cannot Cure Cash Problem

Plan for long-term solutions, not quick fixes, to improve receivables

FIX FOR THE LONG HAUL

First, be of the mindset that whatever you are going to do, it's going to be for the long haul. Take the stance you are going to plan for long-term solutions—not quick fixes to improve the receivables.

A troublesome sign has appeared in recent years as we see hospitals settling too easily and too often for the short-term, quick fix to their cash problem in receivables. There's a small, but concerning trend these days to let someone else into the house to take care of the receivables "problem."

The phrase "early out" is catching on among hospital CFOs and receivables managers. It usually means transferring the account to a third party for collection much earlier than the traditional 120 to 180 days from discharge.

However, the faster transfer to a collection firm outside the hospital doesn't always mean referral to the collection agency approach. It may mean the hospital lets the collection company try to collect self-pay or insurance accounts, but represents itself as the hospital.

In essence, the receivables manager "hires" the outside firm to work the accounts for a fee much less than the traditional 33 percent and does not officially turn the account over to the collection agency.

Quick fixes come under the forms of: hiring outside firms to collect all or most of the receivables; selling or funding the receivables to an outside company; or to basically turn the entire billing and collecting operation over to someone else.

QUICK FIX ONLY IN EXTREME CASES

In our opinion, this kind of quick fix should only be considered if you're in an extremely tight cash-flow pinch, or your receivables are in a horrendous condition and you need to buy some time to get some cash and regroup the department.

Quick fixes are for emergency and short-term only. They are too expensive for the long-haul and they don't help you resolve the real problems causing a cash flow problem, such as lousy management of receivables.

In the long run, you can manage the receivables process much cheaper than any outside firm. Their fees will range anywhere from 6 percent to 12 percent of the dollars collected. This is at least three to six times more expensive than it is for you to do the same thing—assuming you have the management, people and the tools to get the job done right. (There's the rub.)

Plus, nine times out of ten, as soon as the quick fix artists are gone, your cash problems return. They didn't fix the reason they were there in the first place! That's not why they're in business.

The outside firms make profits—big profits—on commissions and fees on dollars collected. And they collect because too often your internal process and staff did such a poor job of collecting in the first place.

Hospitals often add insult to injury and pay a high price for their own incompetence in the management of receivables when they go to the quick fix. And the real causes for the problem never get addressed and corrected.

One quick fix, being sold as the end to all your cash problems is the outsourcing of specific segments of your accounts receivable to an outside firm to perform collection follow-up and collect the cash starting from discharge. These programs should only be considered under the most extreme cash crunch imaginable, and then only for a short time frame. Remember: "The steak does not always taste as good as the sizzle smells." You want to make sure "early out" is not really just an "easy out."

Here are some factors to keep in mind when evaluating these programs with outside firms:

- What will be the initial and ongoing cost of such a program?
- What will be the impact on patient relations?
- What will this outside firm accomplish and why are you unable to achieve the same results?
- What will determine which accounts get referred out?
- Identification of a firm and their services to meet your needs.
- How will the outside firm achieve its goals?
- What will be the time frame for this outside program?
- Will you be able to measure the performance and determine if your goals are being met?

Some experts in the field would argue that these services can provide a valuable complement to your internal staff at the facility. However, the most important points to consider are: 1) control of your accounts, and 2) cost incurred to collect these accounts. These programs do present economies of scale because their cost for computer support is spread over numerous hospitals/clients. However, you lose control, and the programs cost more than if you did it for yourself.

MAKE COST EFFECTIVE DECISIONS

Recent hospital statistics, as reported in the *HARA,* indicate hospitals spend an average of 2.5 cents to collect one dollar in their receivables. Because all outside programs exceed these costs many times over, you have to ask yourself, is it a cost-effective decision to place patient accounts on the outside?

This is how to evaluate the value of an early out:

- Identify segments of your A/R that are not receiving proper collection follow-up.
- Determine the potential dollars that can be collected.
- Evaluate the cost of outside service and relate it to potential collections.
- Compare the cost-effectiveness of an outside service in relation to the cost of internal collection work.
- Determine if the process should proceed or whether you should increase your internal staff and their effectiveness.

Remember: Is it early out or just an easy out?

Another popular quick and expensive fix that hit the industry a couple of years ago was funding or selling of hospital receivables.

You're probably wondering whatever happened to the big hoopla about hospital funding—where hospitals could make their receivables available to "sell" to outside firms and improve their cash position? The answer is, not much.

Firms such as Towers Financial, Shearson Lehman Hutton, Premier Hospital Alliance, Ohio Hospital Association, United Medicorp, CIS and Hospital Billing Collection Services were some of the major players a couple of years ago when hospital receivable funding programs were a hot item.

For whatever reason, the idea is considerably cooler than it was in 1990 when every major trade magazine and newsletter in the business was featuring the hospital receivable funding concept.

Most of the firms that came out strong to market the idea have either dropped the program altogether or modified it to another concept. Based on our research, Towers is one of the few still plugging along with the same concept it started out with a couple of years ago.

United Medicorp, Dallas, was one of the first that came out of the blocks in a big way to finance hospital receivables, but dropped the idea entirely when they ran out of money.

John Muccillo, vice president of sales at United Medicorp said his firm stopped receivables funding in September 1991. Muccillo said, "We got into it because that's how we thought we could see our core business, which is tracking, managing and collecting receivables for hospitals." However, United Medicorp found receivables funding attracted unstable clients. "Many of them were beyond help. Our cash would not save them," Muccillo said.

RECEIVABLES FUNDING TOO EXPENSIVE

Here's a firm that once specialized in receivables funding admitting it was a bad deal for hospitals.

"I do not feel factoring or pre-funding on receivables is a long-term solution to cash flow problems for hospitals. It may be needed for short-term difficulties, such as capital expansion or temporary cash short-falls, but only effective collection procedures can ensure the long-term financial health of any hospital," Muccillo said.

In addition, "Receivables factoring is some of the most expensive money on the planet," Muccillo told us.

CIS, an electronic claims processing firm, now looks at receivables funding only as an add-on to help sell their billing process. Steve Hoffenberger, chairman of Towers, told us they are still doing receivables funding, but also rely heavily on their collection and claim processing business. He said they presently have over 350 health care funding clients.

I was never sold on the concept of selling receivables. I felt it was too expensive and created a bad marriage between the hospital and the financing firm that could not be dissolved without even more expense.

In addition, I feel receivables funding of this nature only covered up the real problems of managing receivables internally within the hospital. Hospitals who were interested in these programs usually had receivable problems. They looked for a quick and easy fix. It wasn't there.

The answer is not in quick and expensive fixes, but managing better internally. Hopefully, hospitals around the nation will come to that same conclusion.

Plan for a permanent solution in your receivables, not a quick fix.

5

Develop A Game Plan

Because you have so much riding on the successful results in maximizing the potential from the receivables, it makes good sense to develop some strategy, a definitive game plan of sorts.

RECEIVABLES IMPROVEMENT PLAN

Because you have so much riding on the successful results in maximizing the potential from the receivables, it makes good sense to develop some strategy, a definitive game plan of sorts.

So, hot button No. 1 is: Spend time to develop a sound, strategic plan to improve the cash from receivables. Get the receivable manager's input, but be sure to give the thought process and planning a good amount of your own time. You have too much at stake to allow others complete control over planning.

This initial plan can cover a short (6 months) or long (one to two years) time frame. I would suggest the shorter approach to start. As you develop your plan, zero in on areas where you can make immediate adjustments. Analysis of the payment history can reveal areas needing attention and pinpoint problems.

A payment history analysis gives direction to collection efforts. Make an analysis of the payment patterns within the major financial classes that make up your accounts receivable. For instance, such financial classes would include: Blue Cross, Medicare, HMOs, Medicaid, commercial insurance and patient pay.

A staff employee can compile the payment history analysis data for each financial class by filling in information from individual accounts after they have been paid. Compiling data on 100 accounts in each financial class should give a good picture. Column headings should include patient, admission date, discharge date, dates of insurance billing and first insurance paid, and insurance company. Information also must provide the date the patient paid, the amount the patient paid at discharge and the total bill.

After a summary has been made of the data and an analysis of the major areas, you can determine what action will increase collection totals and which of the financial classes to target for the big push.

The review may bring surprises: billings not sent out on a timely basis, poor collection activity and follow-up, two or three commercial insurance companies held up most of the money in that category, or accounts sent to the collection agency without enough effort.

Some of the problems may be internal, such as poor staffing, uneven work flow and procedures not followed or updated.

You now have an overall, objective database from which to develop priorities. You can now concentrate on solutions for the quickest results. These might include clearing up a backlog of billing, supplementing staff, collecting at discharge, increasing action from a few commercial companies, decreasing the time before collection starts and collecting more efficiently from outpatient/emergency room accounts.

With the payment history analysis, you can develop a game plan, set new standards and determine a general method of attack for the entire staff.

Key factors in accounts receivable analysis

1. Perform various types of analysis for a wider picture.
2. Determine staff strengths and weaknesses.
3. Determine procedure and policy loopholes.
4. Gain understanding and knowledge of major problems.

If you're looking to develop a plan of attack to try to improve the cash in a relatively short period of time, here's an action plan prototype we use in consulting with hospitals.

OVERVIEW OF A CASH IMPROVEMENT PLAN

For the accounts receivable improvement project to proceed smoothly, your action plan might be divided into four major phases:

First phase: **Reorganization, planning, preparation and set up (First 60 days)**

This 60-day phase involves detailed and careful planning for the improved approach to managing receivables. A new collection process could be designed to include a reorganization, and new policies and procedures. In addition, job descriptions and individual and management reports will be planned. After preparation and design, these management tools will be ready for the training in phase two.

Second phase: Training and development
(From 30- through 90-day period)
This 60-day phase will link training and development to the plans created in the first phase. Detailed procedure, process, collection and human relations training are provided for the business office admitting/registration staff. This second phase could begin midway during the first phase.

Third phase: Implementation
(From 90- through 120-day period)
Starting at 90 days, implementation of the improved approach to managing receivables takes place.

Fourth phase: Monitoring and adjusting the collection process as needed
This fourth phase will connect all activities planned through the first three phases on a monthly basis. Tracking and monitoring of key indicators will take place. Any adjustments to the plan will be made as needed.

Implementation schedule

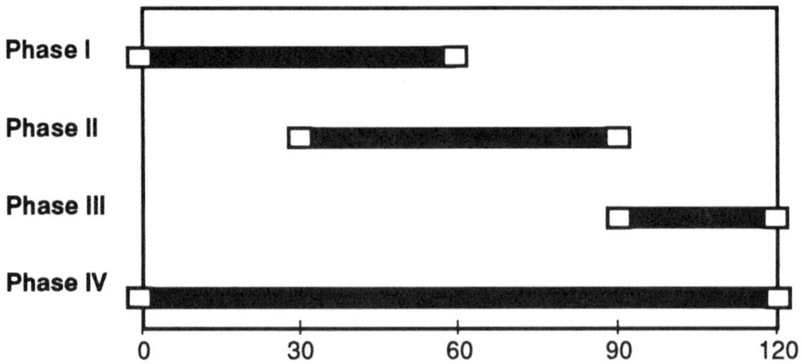

When putting your game plan together, sometimes it helps to see what others did to improve their cash from improved management of receivables.

Mt. Sinai Medical Center, a 600-bed facility in Miami Beach, Fla., is one of those hospitals that has performed a recent financial turnaround. In the process, they have developed some higher standards of excellence and have become a role model for others to follow. Take a look at these figures that cover a span of more than five years and measure a spectacular level of improvement in their receivables.

MOUNT SINAI MEDICAL CENTER RECEIVABLES IMPROVEMENT RESULTS

	Fiscal year 1986	Fiscal year 1991
Gross days revenue outstanding[1]	120	37.9
Bad debt	$16.7 million	$ 4.0 million
Charity	$ 9.0 million	$ 9.6 million
Total uncompensated care	$25.7 million	$13.6 million
Gross revenue	$195.3 million	$338.2 million
Net revenue	$115.3 million	$156.9 million
Contractual write-off (% of gross revenue)	27.8 %	49.6%
Uncompensated care write-off		
Gross revenue	13.2%	4.0%
Net revenue	22.3%	8.7%

[1] Contractual allowances are removed from discharged receivables.

I've decided to highlight only some of the major points behind their dramatic improvement. The thought was, you might see some tips that would be of some help in your own planning...steps they took which you could emulate.

Emulating starts with the people who gave impetus to the improvement—and their attitude. Attitude of the leaders is an underlying factor in any major accomplishment. The major catalyst behind the improvement in this case was Larry Hudson, the hospital CFO. When we asked Hudson about the financial impact of the receivables turnaround, he told us, "Impact of the turnaround? I think it's pretty impressive. If you need evidence, look at this drop in uncompensated care. In 1986, we wrote off $16.7 million in bad debt. Last year, it was $4 million. That's almost $13 million that will go straight to the bottom line."

Actually, if they had kept writing off bad debt at the same percentage of net revenue in 1991 as they had in 1986, the bad debt would have been $23 million, or a difference of $19 million to the bottom line.

Hudson's strength of character and strong desire to excel were obvious when he told us, "I want Mt. Sinai to be the leader—not just in Florida, but nationally. Quite honestly, I think we're better than the competition. I'm out to prove it."

Hudson has this message for his fellow CFOs, "I want my counterparts in the industry to know you don't have to settle for mediocrity. If you expect the best—DEMAND IT. You'll get it."

SIX KEY FACTORS IN IMPROVEMENT PLAN AT MOUNT SINAI

1. **Found a key person for the business office (catalyst).** "Then we didn't throttle (or coddle) the individual. If he or she has got what it takes, the job will get done."

2. **Revamped data processing.** "They had forgotten they were a service unit. We set up an entirely new patient accounting system ("homegrown" Unisys SMSII database), and recruited a new information systems director."
3. **Started re-organization at the beginning (admitting).** "We were determined to get the information right on the front end, and then work our way through the entire cycle."
4. **Hired more collectors.** "We had three in 1986. Now, we have 11."
5. **Provided support.** "The business office needed cooperation from all areas (data processing, medical records, human resources). I saw it as my job to see that they got it."
6. **Worked hard at providing motivation.** "I think it is absolutely essential to recognize the contribution of individuals to the team effort."

So, after you've determined to go for the long-term solution to improve the management of your receivables, put a game plan together to maximize a good, steady cash flow.

6

Keep It Simple

Look at the process as managing the life cycle of your receivables

KEEP LIFE CYCLE SHORT

As a senior executive looking at improving your cash flow and profit by improved management of the receivables, my advice is: **Keep it simple**.

Besides, it simply isn't that complicated anyway. We all have a tendency to overstate the complexity of today's health care reimbursement and management of receivables. It's become much more perplexing in recent years, but it's not an overly complicated process.

The idea is for senior executives not to clutter their minds and get buried in detail in the attempt to improve their receivables. Keep the focus simple and progress easy to track.

Look at receivables as having a "life cycle." That's really

what it's all about. The receivables have a "life" with several stages. The objective is to get through these stages as quickly as possible.

In fact, the life cycle of the receivables begins before any charges are even put on a patient's account and continues through the paid-in-full status.

The key to improving cash flow is to be sure there is enough focus at the key stages of the life cycle of receivables. The question is, where to focus? As a senior executive, where will you get the biggest bang for your buck?

If you stand back and look at the process in its simplest terms, you would identify just four major stages of activity necessary for you to focus on for improvements.

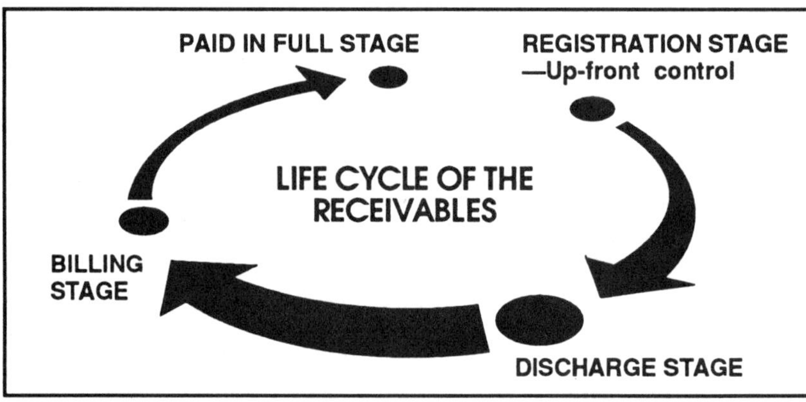

Look at it this way:

LIFE CYCLE OF THE RECEIVABLES

Focus on the four major stages in the aging process

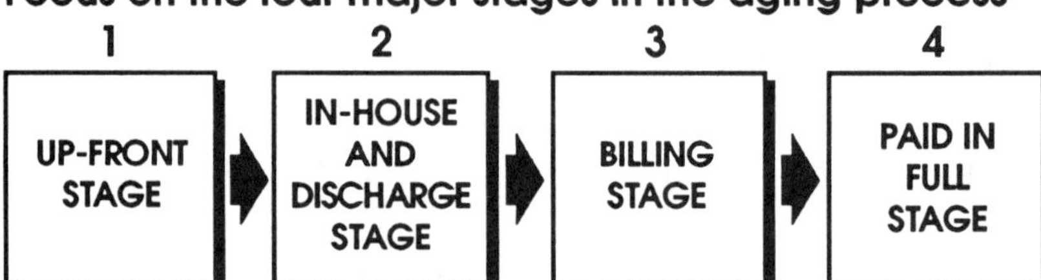

Stage one: Involves all of the admitting and registration areas. Insist on quality information and a quality staff in the admission process.

The function of improving days outstanding is greatly enhanced by the acquisition and subsequent use of accurate general, insurance and financial patient data.

One key element to reducing your days revenue outstanding and improving cash flow is what you do before the inpatient is admitted, or prior-to-service. You need a good preregistration or preadmission system. The system becomes the cornerstone of a successful collection program. This allows for strong patient communication and improved patient relations, resulting in better collection totals.

Expect your admitting staff to preadmit a high percent of the non-emergency inpatient admissions. Track the percentages on an ongoing basis and have them report the results regularly. Also, insist on a low error ratio on patient information. Ask your managers to develop an information quality control process and report error ratios on a regular basis.

Don't tolerate careless work by the registration staff that will create costly delays in reimbursement. Let them know you expect near perfect information in these areas.

Stage two: Includes the activity that takes place during the inpatient's stay and at the point of discharge. Because the vast majority of your cash will come through inpatient revenue, you will want to tighten up all the controls prior to the patient leaving the hospital.

Close control of account balances while patients are hospitalized will help reduce large balance surprises. But, tight control of the payment or arrangements of the patient's portion of the bill *after the service has been rendered* will go a long way toward keeping the self-pay portion of your receivables where you want them.

It is a "last chance" situation. The last convenient opportunity to complete the records with information not previously secured. It is the first opportunity to place a bill before the patient and to attempt to collect that part of the bill which is the patient's responsibility.

Require all inpatients to stop at the cashier office prior to discharge so that patients can be counseled about their portion of the bill. Forget the courtesy discharge process. Practically every one of your inpatients will owe something today with the increase in deductibles and co-pay.

STRIKE WHEN PATIENT COOPERATION HIGHEST

In addition, a good inpatient discharge system obtains cooperation from patients when their cooperation level is the highest. The chart below shows the collection psychological advantage is best prior to an inpatient's discharge. After discharge, the psychological advantage the hospital had is lost. The point should be obvious.

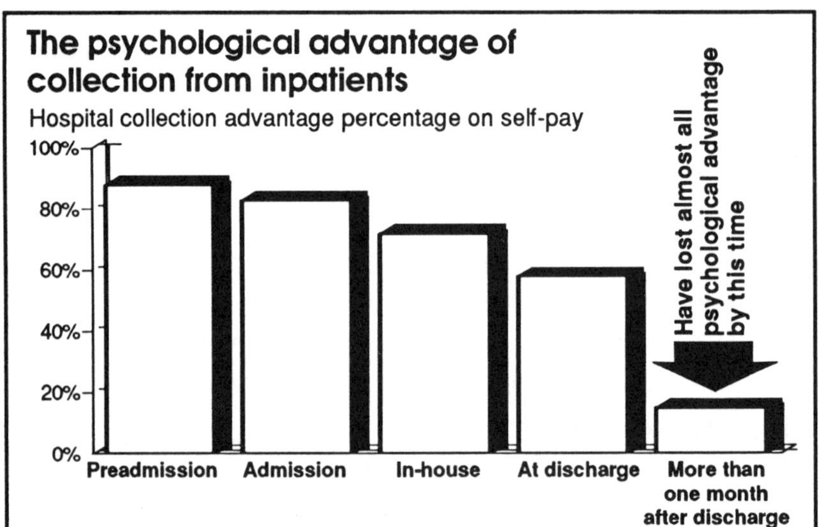

Focus on staffing qualified cashiers and financial counselors with tight controls and reports during this stage.

Stage three: Focuses on all aspects of billing the third-party insurance and the patient. Again, staffing, automation, accuracy and speed in getting the bills out are critical in this stage. Develop standards of excellence in quality and quantity billed, with high expectations in terms of how fast and accurate bills leave the house. Require tracking and regular reports on performance from the receivables manager on all activity that falls into this stage. Provide state of the art automated claims processing for your business office.

Stage four: This is everything that is left over from the previous three stages—but primarily getting the bills into a "paid-in-full" status as quickly as possible. This usually includes all of the collection follow-up activity.

This stage of the life cycle is where most hospitals fail miserably. Their collection follow-up units are understaffed, underqualified, lack training and operate without the automation that enhances performance.

Look to build up the effectiveness of your business office staff within this stage. Insist on qualified people with collection experience. Staff the unit properly and provide the best automated collection follow-up system available for your situation. Your return on investment will be fast and multiplied many times over.

For the most part, the remaining chapters will cover various aspects which impact each of these four stages in the life cycle of receivables.

If you keep it simple by focusing on improving the performance on the activity that takes place in these areas, with the objective and high expectations of maintaining a very short life cycle of your receivables, you'll improve cash flow considerably.

7

Improve and Increase Automation

One of the major areas for senior executives to focus their attention is the amount of state-of-the-art automation in the management of receivables.

NEED MORE AUTOMATION IN RECEIVABLES

One of the major areas for senior executives to focus their attention on is the amount of state of the art automation in the management of receivables. Automation needs your attention, because most existing hospital patient account systems are underutilized or antiquated by today's needs.

Excellent automated systems can cut huge time chunks in the turnaround of your cash. It can also provide tremendous savings in labor costs in the business office. Bad systems, on the other hand, can kill you.

Hot button No. 2: Give automation in the business office prime-time attention. It's one of the keys to improving cash flow.

The U.S. Health and Human Services Department estimates

more than 6 billion medical claims were generated in 1991. That's enough paperwork to completely bury most of the nation's hospital billing and collection departments. It often does.

While automation strides have been taken in the past decade to improve cash flow and speed up the reimbursement process, the hospital industry is nowhere near where it needs to be. The industry has improved its technology, but it's only beginning to scratch the surface. Your hospital is probably no exception.

ADVANTAGES OF AUTOMATION

A few hospitals are discovering the advantages of total and state of the art automation—primarily electronic billing and collection follow-up systems. Some are reluctant to change, and some settle for a less than effective system. For example, the concept of electronic claims processing is by no means new and most hospitals now electronically bill Medicare and the Blues. But the idea has been a part of the business world for more than 20 years.

Electronic claims processing typically works by sending billing data through a modem and a dedicated telephone line. The information is transmitted directly to the respective payer or to a clearinghouse, which processes the data and sends it electronically to the proper payer. Clearinghouses generally charge a fee for processing the information. But some software programs are far superior to others and allow the user to bypass the services and send the information directly to the payer.

Cleaner, more efficient claims, prompter payment and reduced staff should be enough of an incentive to inspire most hospital CEOs and CFOs to consider the advantages of electronic claims processing for all claims. But even in electronic billing, problems will exist if the information going into the system is bad.

Richard E. Johnson, policy analyst with the American Hospital Association says far too much time is being wasted by hospitals that send out bills only to have them rejected because some small piece of information was either not included, or simply submitted in the wrong format. Too often a provider must first send out a cancellation of the old, incorrect bill and wait for it to be processed before the new, corrected bill can be sent out.

There still is no substitute for excellence in quality.

In addition to saving tremendous amounts of time in the billing office, electronic billing also eliminates postage and manual handling costs. It also eliminates many human errors as a result of limited human intervention. Today, claims can be electronically submitted for most medical procedures being billed to the Blues as well as most other payers, including most of the major commercials and managed care policies.

For the potential buyer, the world of electronic claims processing can best be described as "confusing." This is because the marketplace has quite a variety of products for different services and prices. Our research shows there are upwards of 200 companies offering some part of electronic claims processing. Just *what* they *can* do gets even more confusing. Most of the companies are marketing software providing an electronic format for paper claims.

MAJOR CLASSIFICATIONS

If you want to understand the electronic claims processing industry, it is best to begin with some knowledge of the *major classifications* of companies providing electronic claims processing services:

1. **Clearinghouses.** These firms represent hospitals as an "*interface other.*" They view their role as problem solvers, fixing

claims provided by accounts receivable software—NEIC, CIS, SSI, for example.

2. **Software vendors.** These companies are hospital information system vendors who got into electronic claims processing as an offshoot of patient accounting affiliations. These software vendors are represented by the national companies: HBO, SMS, Spectrum, etc. Increasingly, they offer services similar to the clearinghouse vendors (in response to demand from other hospitals).
3. **The Blues.** Just about every Blue Cross/Blue Shield plan offers some form of electronic claims processing. Some have spun off with sophisticated for-profit subsidiaries, while others offer only limited data processing assistance, limited help and should not be considered with the "big boys."
4. **Third-party carriers.** There are over 1,500 health insurance carriers and benefit plans. Most of the big-time plans work through KNACK (a clearinghouse). However, over 1,000 commercial plans do not work through KNACK.

The *HARA (Hospital Accounts Receivables Analysis)*, put out quarterly by Zimmerman & Associates Inc., consistently shows that health care providers are overwhelmed by account volume. In fact, the average health care collector in a hospital averages more than 4,000 active accounts. This means hospitals nationwide are looking at ways to improve personalized patient contact. Some are opting for follow-up collection systems to solve this problem.

CONSIDER AUTOMATED COLLECTION FOLLOW-UP SYSTEM

In an effort to improve cash flow and handle collection problems related to an increase in self-pay, some hospitals are going to automated collection systems, and many more need to consider this aspect of automation. If you are over 125 beds, so should you.

Both vendors of the collection system and financial managers sing high praises of the automation of collection activity. While these systems are not new to retail credit, banks and collection agencies, they are new to the health care industry. Unfortunately, a recent survey[1] shows less than 13 percent of hospitals have a "paperless" automated collection system.

These new systems are called "paperless" because the collection staff uses computer screens to collect—not paper. They all aim to: 1) automate the manual work involved in collection, 2) help organize the collector, 3) put the collector in touch with more people, and 4) provide better performance reports.

While few hospital financial managers have the luxury of an automated collection system for their collection staff, most feel it will be one of the major reasons they have any chance for improving days and bad debt.[2] Here's an example where an automated follow-up system paid dividends:

Until recently, All Saints Episcopal Hospital in Fort Worth, Texas, had been working with a system that was 100 percent manual. The staff of seven collectors routinely sat at desks literally buried beneath mountains of paperwork. Good collection follow-up was "virtually impossible," Bill Kennedy, the hospital's director of business services told me.

Receivables days hovered in the upper 70s between two All Saints campuses. Kennedy went with a follow-up collection system provided by Ontario Systems out of Muncie, Ind. In less than six months, Kennedy saw his days dip to about 55.

---

[1] Zimmerman & Associates, Inc., *HARA (Hospital Accounts Receivable Analysis)*, 1992.

[2] See note 1 above.

Not every hospital that has switched to an automatic follow-up collection system has enjoyed the same success as Kennedy. There are some horror stories of hospitals that purchased a system and found it fell short of what the vendor had promised, or the staff was not trained to use it properly.

"It's a jungle of systems out there!" That's how one health care receivables expert described the current marketplace for computerized collection systems and software. Vendors who have been serving collection agencies are extremely anxious to capture the growing market for automated collection software in hospitals and hospital-owned agencies.

SORT OUT THE SYSTEMS AVAILABLE

We have some suggestions to help you sort out the "jungle" of automated collection systems. For starters, decide which of the many solutions out there is right for you...*a stand-alone system, which operates independently as a back-end to your patient accounting system, or one which is an integral part of your patient accounting system.* If you buy a stand-alone system, make sure it will provide for easy flow of information between patient accounting and collection.

You also have the option of: 1) buying or leasing the system and software and operating as a turnkey configuration or, 2) contracting for service and support on a contingency basis. (The latter option is especially appealing if your budget fails to allow for an outright capital expenditure, but you'll have to share the profits.)

No matter which route you take, you will need to ask the following questions:

1. How flexible is the software? Will it adapt to your hospital's collection philosophy and priorities? Does it provide follow-up on insurance accounts as well as self-pay?

2. Is it easy to install? Will it interface with existing hospital hardware and software? If not, will the cost of additional hardware, software and/or interfacing justify your selection? (If you will be purchasing an entire system, be sure the hardware is reliable.) What's the recovery time following a power outage? What are the maintenance costs?
3. What is the vendor's track record? How long have they been in business? How long have they been serving the health care industry? Are they financially viable? How many similar systems have they installed? Will they stay in business over the next five years?
4. What do their customers say? Is the collection system/software cost effective? Was it easy for their employees to learn? How is the support?

CHOOSING A VENDOR

Over 200 software companies offer some form of electronic claims processing to health care providers. Another hundred or so offer follow-up collection systems. Many of the systems being sold by these vendors are relatively similar.

The question really is not **which** system to choose, but rather, which **vendor** will best meet the needs of your facility.

Selecting the right system for your facility can be a very simple process if you take some time and do your homework. Obviously purchasing a billing system is a little different than buying a new car. There's more to it than finding one that's the right color and in your price range.

The first step is to take a good look at the systems available to you. I must admit, a good place to start is a new and informative guide to automated follow-up collection, electronic billing and patient accounting systems. These special reports, published in 1993 by Zimmerman & Associates Inc., list more than 100 vendors with systems in operation around the country.

The guides list information about each system's features, price, required hardware and software, amount of training required and the estimated time to install it. The guide also includes comments from people who already have put these systems to the test.

Most vendors can supply you with a list of their current clients. Talk to these people and find out what they like and don't like about the systems. More importantly, find out how quickly the vendor responds when something goes wrong.

Talking to people who have been in the same boat as you will keep you from capsizing. It also will give you an idea of where your budget should be. Be sure the people you contact operate a facility similar in size and specialty to your own. A system that works perfectly for a small clinic could well be a disaster for a hospital.

After discussing various systems with your colleagues, it shouldn't take long to narrow your selection to a handful of vendors. Take the time to get to know each one and discuss what they have to offer. It's easy to be lured in by a system which offers a lot of bells and whistles. Check the track record of each vendor being considered. You're taking a risk to go with a vendor who has been in the business less than five years.

Next, make certain you know exactly what you want your system to accomplish. Talk to the people who will be using the system on a daily basis. They are the ones who really have a feel for what the system should be able to do. Let your business office staff have some input in your decision-making process. Your team will be more receptive to working with a system that they feel they helped choose.

CIS, a claims processing vendor based in Tulsa, Okla.,

targets individual hospitals with 100 or more beds, and hospital systems. Their electronic billing systems offer customization, on-line editing and toll-free support. The system generally takes no more than 90 days to install and training is included in the package price of about $30,000. CIS also has its own clearinghouse and works with hospitals in all 50 states.

Another of the large vendors is Phoenix, Ariz.-based GTE Health Systems. GTE has more than 50 hospital clients with nearly 15,000 provider offices. Rather than charging a flat fee for the system, GTE charges roughly $0.40 for each claim processed. GTE also has locations nationwide.

Don't judge a vendor by size alone however. Houston-based Electronic Claims Services is a small vendor when compared to giants like GTE and CIS, but the company is establishing an excellent reputation. To date, ECS only has 35 hospital or clinic clients, all of which are in Texas or New Mexico. Their all-payer electronic billing system works with Medicare, Medicaid, Champus, the Blues and other commercial payers.

CHECKLIST FOR BUYING AUTOMATION

For someone shopping around for a new or improved system, there are a number of things to consider.

1. **Set your objectives.** Decide exactly what you want the system to accomplish. The time to make the decision to purchase an electronic billing and collecting system is when you see your present system becoming too cumbersome.
2. **Beware of hidden costs.** About 20 percent of your budget will be spent on hidden costs such as backup disks, ribbons, paper, furniture and general supplies. Find out what the price of an average service call is, and check the vendor's record. Check with others who have the system as to what

their maintenance costs are. Maintenance costs are a good indicator of hardware reliability. How quickly can your vendor correct a problem? What about on nights and weekends?

3. **The system should be compatible with other types of hardware and be able to use a variety of software.** It should be easily updated, and be able to integrate with other systems.
4. **Your vendor should have a verifiable track record.** Be leery of any vendor who has been in the business for less than five years. Talk to people who are using the system to find out what they really think of it. Try to discover any shortcomings which your vendor may have neglected to mention.
5. **Technical support as well as efficient response time is important.** Can your vendor be reached 24 hours a day?
6. **Does the vendor supply ample training** for the people who will be using the system? If your people don't find it easy to operate, they will be reluctant to use it. This will render an extremely expensive system virtually worthless.
7. **The software should be menu-driven and user-friendly.** Your software should incorporate a lot of help screens so your employees don't have to continually consult a manual.
8. **Most systems are compatible with Medicare, but look for a system that is flexible** enough to work with a variety of contract arrangements.
9. **Make sure the system, including all of necessary software, is within your budget.**
10. **The system should allow you to jump easily from file to file,** without having to continually enter a patient's name or identification number. How easy is it to add information to an existing file?
11. **The system should allow for easy follow-ups** once billing

has been sent out.

12. **It's the worker bees who really understand what a system needs to be able to do. Get everyone involved in the decision-making process.** Your workers will be much more receptive to learning a system if they know they had a hand in choosing it.

8

EDI Will Revolutionize the Billing Process

Electronic Data Interchange will allow for billing and payment to be entirely electronic by 1996.

BIG CHANGES

As we go to press with this book, there's an electric storm brewing in hospital billing and payment. Get your umbrellas out, because it's going to "rain change!" Serious change.

Something called EDI, Electronic Data Interchange, will revolutionize the way health care claims are processed. For example, by 1996 at the latest, the entire industry will receive all reimbursements electronically. This is also part of President Clinton's plan to reduce costs in the industry.

Essentially, it will work like this: The patient will come into your facility with an identification card and your registration staff will do a card swipe. The card swipe information will then go to the insurance company where the benefits will be verified, and verification will be sent back electronically to the hospital.

As a part of that electronic process, the billing will be sent electronically to the third-party payer, who in turn will send the payment back electronically to the provider, or it will be posted electronically. In addition, the collection follow-up reports will be sent out automatically, and utilization review in case management issues will be done electronically with the insurance company.

As we see it now, the insurance companies, as part of this EDI deal, will agree to not request so much information from the providers. In other words, they are going to have to trust the hospitals.

SUPPORTED BY INSURANCE COMPANIES

Now why in the world would the insurance companies agree to this? One simple reason. They're frightened of national health insurance. In other words, the payer is, at this point, willing to play ball with the hospitals and clinics. EDI is being strongly supported by insurance companies. But why would payers be in support of a system which would make them pay their bill faster?

John H. St. George, director of patient financial services at Mary Hitchcock Memorial Hospital in Hanover, N.H., believes insurance companies are worried the government will step in if they don't begin showing some improvements to the health care industry. Insurers realize that if a national health care system were to be put in place, many of them would be out of business. Payers also will be able to tell the banks exactly when to release the funds to pay a particular bill.

Hospitals, not surprisingly, are very concerned about having a new standard of billing forced upon them, according to Richard Johnson, a policy analyst with the American Hospital Association. Many are worried the cost of installing new hardware and software will fall on their shoulders. At this point, it's really a moot discussion. The industry is going electronic and hospitals must be prepared to meet it head on.

Right now, there's a process in place through the American National Standards Institute, otherwise known as the ANSI. They have a group of providers and insurance companies working together to develop EDI standards. The sad thing is, as far as we can see at the conferences we attend, there are few health care providers and hospitals in attendance. The hospital industry may be asleep at the switch right now in terms of the ANSI process.

Administrative savings is the buzzword going around today for reducing costs in health care. Electronic Data Interchange is seen as a sure-fire way to create tangible results.

The Workgroup for Electronic Data Interchange (WEDI) recently released a report on implementing an electronic claims standard. Members of the workgroup estimate adopting a national standard for billing could cut the nation's health care bill by as much as $10 billion annually.

The group, which was formed by the U.S. Department of Health and Human Services, represents public and private health care providers and payers. The group was formed to examine the possibility of creating uniform, computerized billing standards and increasing electronic claims submission. The standards are being devised by the ANSI.

UNIFORM STANDARDS IN PLACE BY 1996

WEDI is urging all participants in the health care industry to adopt a uniform standard for major business transactions. Major players are expected to be using the new standards by the fourth quarter of 1994; all other participants, two years later.

Today, virtually every electronic form that is sent out by a hospital uses a different format and contains different pieces of information. Under the EDI plan, a hospital would use one format for all of its major billing.

This, theoretically, will lead to a faster exchange of data, less paperwork and lower administrative costs. It's not nearly as easy as it sounds however. Getting providers, as well as payers, from each state to agree on a uniform system could be a real challenge.

As you're looking toward the future, you will see that business office and claims processing people are targeting two-thirds reduction in staffing to bring down the administrative costs of producing claims by about one-third. Your business office of the future, in the near future—will be a shell of what it is now.

The main functions of the business office will be collection follow-up, working on claims that are not paid and that can't be done electronically, and collecting from patients. The other important part of the business office function will be patient public relations—and that will take on increased importance.

One further note, the Employee Retirement Income Security Act allows some employers to be self-insured and not follow the laws of the insurance commissioner. As part of this EDI process, ERISA must be changed so that self-insured companies also have to play ball electronically. In other words, for quite some time, the self-paid insurance companies have been able to get out of processing claims like regulated insurance companies. As part of the EDI process, they will need to reform ERISA laws so that self-insured companies also have to play ball electronically. That will level the playing field for everyone.

9

Maximize Utilization of Your Automated Patient Accounting System

Too often taken for granted, there's a good chance your present system is not being utilized to its' maximum possibility in managing the receivables.

PRESENT SYSTEMS SELDOM FULLY UTILIZED

A key factor to improving cash flow is the improved utilization of the automated patient accounting system you are using. Too often taken for granted, there's a good chance your present system is not being utilized to its potential in managing the receivables.

Most hospital business offices don't properly utilize their automated patient accounting systems. That's the conclusion I draw from talking to hospital data processing managers and vendors.

I recently attended a presentation by Cam Graham, HBO & Company and Kevin Hunt, Concord Hospital, Concord, NH. The seminar covered the need for patient accounting departments to review the information and systems that they currently have available to them.

One interesting statistic presented was the result of a survey of hospital data processing professionals. The question asked was, "What will be their primary challenge over the next two years?" Nearly 50 percent responded, "the integration of existing applications", and 27 percent responded, "increasing the use and acceptance of applications." This means that over 75 percent of the respondents believe their systems are underutilized.

Because this aspect of improving cash is so critical to your success, I strongly suggest you take time to audit the utilization of your patient accounting system. Check for use of all reports by the staff. Look at the billing cycle process for effectiveness. Talk to your business office staff. What do they like about the system and what are their complaints? Do the same in your data processing department. And don't just talk to the managers and supervisors. You'll probably get more frank responses from the grass roots employees.

Once you've completed your analysis, bring your staff together to discuss your findings and their recommendations for changes to better utilize your system.

If hospital data processing managers and vendors claim the business office isn't utilizing their system for maximum results, hospital business managers fire right back. It's a common complaint among hospital receivables managers—their patient accounting data processing system is not satisfactory in their minds.

A recent national survey shows over 40 percent of RMs say they are dissatisfied with their DP system.[1]

---

[1] Zimmerman & Associates, Inc., *HARA (Hospital Accounts Receivable Analysis)*, 1992.

REASONS MANAGERS NOT HAPPY WITH SYSTEM

As we see it, there are four major reasons why patient accounting systems are not meeting the needs of RMs:

1. **Uninformed users** While it's easy to blame data processing, you also have to look inward. Is the business office staff intimate with your system? Can you adjust billing profiles as needed? Your staff should know what the system can do for them before they blame "the system" for all their problems.

   We see this as the No. 1 reason managers are dissatisfied. They are uninformed users. We see examples of it all the time in our consulting projects.
2. **System support** Today's sophisticated data processing systems require top-notch support. The truth is, many do not get it. Your billing problems don't make the "priority list" (but a nursing request does). Good data processing programmers and support are hard to find, if you've got them, it's all too rare. It's a problem with all major vendors.
3. **Hardware limitations** Some of the systems are overloaded. This results in poor response time and/or significant down time. Some of you just don't have enough machine to run a day-to-day patient accounting operation.
4. **Software barriers** This can come in many forms. Vendors are notorious for incomplete releases, and the burden of proof is always on your staff to show why it doesn't work. In addition, many hospitals have "bastardized" their software to meet "unique" needs. These software adjustments come back to haunt the staff on a regular basis.

In today's health care environment, are hospitals providing chief financial officers and receivables managers with the state-of-the-art tools necessary to effectively control their accounts receivable? Here's a better question. With current gross days in receivables at 74 days, do hospitals need to provide more resources to improve the turnaround of these outstanding dollars?

State of the art computer software is required today to ensure solid control of your A/R. It's no longer just nice, it's necessary.

NOT UPGRADING FAST ENOUGH

However, recent survey information released by Sheldon I. Dorenfest & Associates, Ltd., of Chicago, shows the number of hospitals acquiring or upgrading their patient accounting system is declining. During 1988, 9.5 percent of hospitals bought new systems; in 1989, only 8.9 percent of hospitals bought systems. Data for 1990 also reflects similar numbers of purchases as in 1989. This reduction of actual purchases points to less up-to-date computer support for the business office.

Based on a recent Zimmerman & Associates' national survey, only 37 percent of hospitals are even *considering* an automated collection system to complement collection activity. These developments are not encouraging when reviews of numerous business office operations conducted by consultants point to a lack of needed data processing support. To allow for effective control, various data processing support functions are required.

The following computer support is needed to effectively control your A/R:

- Proration of insurance/self-pay portions
- Ability to provide a bill at time of service, at any point of service
- Effective management reports
- Accurate aging of accounts
- Up-to-date, accurate patient information

- Appropriate edits for production of final bills
- On-line comments to record follow-up notes from preadmission to collection follow-up.
- Automated and effective statements/data mailers
- Effective collection follow-up systems
- Electronic billing interface

Here are some examples of innovative exception reporting from data processing that managers find helpful in analyzing receivables:

- Alpha splits by collector, showing aged trial balance and collections by collector, biller, or cashier
- Daily report showing month-to-date collections to goal
- Report performance of collection agency and attorney you use. Include gross and net recovery figures
- ATB by collection agency
- Printout of accounts with collection agency showing only over 90 days with no payment
- Dollars collected at time of service for emergency room and outpatient and at discharge on inpatients
- Bad debt write-off by admitting doctor/by collector
- Accounts held in billing because of delay in medical records and doctor's final diagnosis
- Self-pay installment/contract report
- Financial counselor reports—by collection and aging of their open accounts

  If you are using the financial counselor system of responsibility, each of the counselors should have a separate trial balance including only their accounts. This technique reduces the bulk of the individual reports and serves as a management tool for measuring the counselor's collection effectiveness.

- Ratio of collections of self-pay at time of discharge

- Unbilled status report—by location, financial class and aging
- Deposit record
- Discharge-to-bill status report—by financial class
- Billing report—by financial class, number and dollars
- Average turnaround time by third-party payers
- Write-off to bad debt analysis
- Collection agency results and evaluation
- Employee productivity reports
- Ratio of collection to department expense
- Cost per account to collect (department expenses)
- Summary Analysis Report

REPORTS SHOULD PROVIDE SUMMARIZED ANALYSIS

Finally, the managers should have available, upon request, reports that provide a summarized analysis of receivables. This should show the dollars and, if appropriate, the number of accounts in each aging bracket and in each major financial category. Assuming that revenue figures are maintained by financial class, this allows for each calculation of days outstanding by primary payer, an important factor in determining where the greatest collection efforts should be devoted.

A patient accounting system's ability to provide these resources are essential for you to control your receivables. Today, it would appear that hospitals are either not willing or do not realize that without the investment of appropriate data processing support, their cost of bad debts and uncollectibles will continue to increase.

One constant area of concern for hospitals is the quality of their patient accounting system. The truth is everyone in receivables management can find some fault with their current patient accounting system. After all, if the available patient accounting systems were so good, what need would there be for automated collection follow-up systems and sophisticated electronic billing technology?

For hospitals, the leading systems, SMS, IBAX, American Express, GTE, Meditech, TDS and Gerber Alley, all have strong points and areas where they are not quite as good.

If you're looking for a new system, you need to ask the right questions. Here's a list:

1. *Can I have successful references for this system?* Ask this twice. Here's the trick—get a list of references from your vendor, then cross them all off the list. You know those are reasonably happy clients. Get another list from your vendor. This list should help you talk to clients who are more likely to give you the answers you are looking for. (This doesn't mean the software vendors are not being honest with you. It's a way to talk to users who are not routinely called by prospective clients.)
2. *What's different about your system?* Find out what separates the patient accounting system you are looking at from the others on your list. As you might expect, most of the top vendors are fairly similar for the primary system functions.
3. *How much custom work will it take to get the reports I need?* Most patient accounting vendors will tell you any report "can be programmed." Find out how much work it will take to get the reports you need.
4. *Don't ever ask, "Can your system interface with our other systems?"* Most patient accounting software vendors will say they can interface with other systems, and they probably can, to some degree. Find out what it's *really* going to take to get your system working with other facility systems.
5. *Ask the vendor for their system solution to your operational problems.* Patient accounting software vendors have the advan-

tage of providing solutions based on previous successful experiences. Ask your vendor for their solutions, rather than thinking you already know the answers.

Any hospital receivables manager who thinks they can operate successfully today without at least a working knowledge of computers, better think again. Although it's not necessary they be able to program a computer, at a minimum, they should be able to communicate their needs in terms a data processing professional can understand.

Developing solid computer reports that help control and facilitate the collection process can make the difference between average and superior performance. Don't assume your data systems support staff will understand needs and "magically" provide the receivables manager with the information required to manage the receivables.

It's the responsibility of the receivables manager to define information requirements, and then work with the data processing division to assure the business office staff has the information necessary to achieve success.

It's the CFO's job to see that they do.

10

Unmask the Patient-Pay Phenomenon

Patients now make up a greater portion of a hospital's net revenue than at any time since the early '60s.

UNAWARE OF PHENOMENON

There is a phenomenon going on that is having a subtle but negative impact on cash. That's the phenomenon that patients now make up a greater portion of hospital's net revenue than at any time since the early 1960s.

Our studies indicate over 20 percent of the hospital's net revenue comes directly from the patient.[1] Fifteen years ago, self-pay made up less than 10 percent of net revenue. Increasing deductibles and contractual allowances have changed the percent of patient pay to net revenue dramatically in recent years.

[1] Zimmerman & Associates, Inc., *HARA (Hospital Accounts Receivable Analysis)*, Second Quarter, 1992.

More than 18 percent of the nation's hospitals total accounts receivable outstanding is in patient pay.[2] It ranks right behind Medicare (28 percent) and commercial insurance (19 percent). Unfortunately, more than 30 percent of all the hospital's patient-pay is written off to bad debt. Hospitals under 100 beds write off nearly half of their patient pay to bad debt.[3]

Add to those embarrassing figures charity write-offs, another 18 percent of patient pay revenue.[4] Hospitals in this country are writing off nearly one-half of their extremely profitable patient-pay to bad debt or charity. *Part of the reason is that they simply are not consciously aware of what is going on that causes more patient pay.*

HOSPITALS NOT DEALING WITH PRIVATE-PAY

Perhaps conscious is the wrong word. But hospitals are certainly not dealing with the patient-pay phenomenon. As a result, it slows down their cash and dramatically eats away at their profit.

Because of rising health care costs, most employers in the past 15 years have dropped the old 100 percent reimbursement for hospitals and surgical care, increased the deductibles, and set workers' annual out-of-pocket maximums in excess of $1,000.

Those are among the alarming trends between the early 1980s and now, according to a survey of 560 major employers by Hewitt Associates, a Lincolnshire, Ill.-based benefits consulting firm. Annual deductibles for individual coverage generally rose over 100 percent or more since 1985.

[2] Zimmerman & Associates, Inc., *HARA (Hospital Accounts Receivable Analysis)*, Second Quarter, 1992.

[3] See note 2 above.

[4] See note 2 above.

What can you expect to happen with insurance benefits in the near future?

With health care costs getting major attention from all employers around the nation, most are scrambling to find a "formula" that will reduce their cash layout for employee health insurance coverage. Health care benefits will probably get a major shake up over the next five years with this "formula."

A recent issue of *Business and Health* looks at what companies say they'll be doing to cut future health care costs. The news in a nutshell: Patients will be made to pay more money for fewer benefits.

Take retirees, for example. In a survey by Hewitt Associates, 64 percent of employers surveyed plan to make one or more changes to their retiree health benefits coverage within two years. Of the survey respondents, 45 percent say they'll increase the retiree contribution for current retirees. What about future retirees and people yet to be hired? The percentages go even higher, up to 61 percent and 60 percent respectively.

Companies' long-range planning bodes even more benefits shrinkage. Sixty-two percent of firms say they "definitely will consider" increasing retiree contributions over the next five years, while 39 percent say they'll consider tying retiree contributions to length of service. A scant 5 percent of respondents say they'll consider dropping retiree medical coverage altogether.

In the medical cost area, trends are going in only one direction—up, with the only variable being the rate of increase. For overall national health expenditures, the rate of increase seems to be slowing. Among employers, annual cost increases seem to have stabilized at around 10.3 percent.

What are employers doing about this? More employers of all sizes are self-insuring, with the biggest increase between 1986 and 1989 among employers with 10,000 or more employees.

In a recent survey, employers said they would increase employee co-payments (37 percent), increase deductibles (33 percent) and reduce benefits (12 percent).[5] Look for deductibles and co-pay to continue to inflate your self-pay receivables and contribute to increased bad debt

DEDUCTIBLES WILL CONTINUE TO INCREASE

According to the Hay Group, Inc., in Washington, D.C., employers are continuing to increase employee deductibles.

Cost containment approaches, 1980-1992

	Percentage of companies reporting			
	1980	1985	1990	1991
Cost shifting				
Employee contribution required				
Single premium	32	39	51	55
Family premium	60	65	75	77
Employee deductible greater than 150	0	19	43	49
Hospital coverage reimbursed at less than 100%	27	41	53	58
Pay-based cost sharing[6]	—	—	1	3
Health promotion				
Health promotion plan in effect	—	57	81	82
Financial incentives for wellness	—	—	—	9
Flexible benefits				
Flexible benefits	—	8	14	14
Choice of indemnity medical coverage	—	9	23	25
Flexible spending accounts	—	16	57	68

[6] Something new that a handful of companies are doing is what we can call 'pay-based' cost sharing. Here, the company deductible (or premium contribution, or out-of-pocket limits) may be expressed as a percentage of pay—thus giving lower-paid employees less of a burden than those who are higher paid. Another way this can work is to create tiers. For instance: those making less than $15,000 per year pay a $100 deductible; those between $15,000 and $25,000 might pay a $200 deductible; $25,000-plus might top out at a $300 deductible.

Source: The Hay Group Inc. 1992

[5] The Olsten Corporation, Westbury, N.Y., 1992. Poll of 595 companies. Respondents could choose more than one answer.

Nearly 50 percent of the employers surveyed now have employee deductibles greater than $150 and nearly 60 percent have hospital coverage reimbursed at less than 100 percent.

As those deductibles increase, don't look for self-pay collections to get any easier in the next few years. There are enough ill-winds in the air to forecast tough sledding in collecting from patients for some time.

Here are some highlights of the writing on the wall that spells cash problems for hospitals in the next several years.

- **Number of jobless left without benefits**

  The number of workers in the United States who have exhausted their jobless benefits and are ineligible for further assistance is still high, according to the Labor Department.

  Officials said that over 355,000 workers nationwide have used up their unemployment benefits at the end of October, 1992. The nation's unemployment rate hit an eight-year high of 7.8 percent in mid-'92.

- **Personal savings flat**

  Most people aren't saving as much these days. The nation's percent of disposable personal income has taken a dip in recent years.

  There's little comfort to be found in an article in the latest *Brookings Papers on Economic Activity* by Barry Bosworth and Gary Burtless, of the Brookings Institution, and John Sabelhaus, of Towson State University in Baltimore. Their analysis of government surveys of household savings behavior in recent decades not only rejects most of the popular explanations of the savings drop, but suggest that the most likely cause offers scant hope for a savings revival.

- **Bankruptcies on record pace**

  More than one million American consumers and businesses

will likely file for bankruptcy this year, with the heaviest filings coming from economically shellshocked New England, the American Bankruptcy Institute reported recently.

"The number of bankruptcies is increasing in an unbroken string and at record pace," said Samuel J. Gerdano, executive director of the Institute, a non-profit group whose members include lawyers, accountants and others in the bankruptcy industry.

Patients probably tell your business office cashiers and financial counselors they can't pay their portion of the bill. They probably are telling the truth, because they most likely will be up to their eyeballs in debt on their credit cards and there will be no "room" for your bill. The American public charged over $350 billion on credit and charge cards last year—more than what was spent on all of the nation's hospital charges last year. Can you believe that?

MANY HOSPITALS DON'T IDENTIFY PATIENT'S PORTION

Compounding this problem of self-pay is the fact that many hospitals do not utilize their patient accounting system properly and therefore cannot even identify the patient's portion of the total bill until the insurance pays. They can't make financial arrangements with the patient when he leaves the hospital as an inpatient. Moreover, they can't even bill the patient for his portion until the insurance pays—anywhere from 30 to 90 days after discharge.

In addition, those hospital aging of accounts receivable computer reports do not reflect true dollars outstanding in any of the financial classes. They are constantly looking at bad numbers. It's been around forever, but some 50 percent of the nation's hospitals still don't use proration.[7] (Check to see if

[7] Zimmerman & Associates, Inc., *HARA (Hospital Accounts Receivable Analysis)*, 1992.

this is the case in your hospital.) Proration is simply verifying insurance benefits, and then estimating how much the patient owes. Then, inform the patient of what they owe as early as possible.

Surprisingly, this easy process is not used by everyone.

If you don't use proration, there is no way to know how much is owed from patients. According to the Health Care Financing Administration, in 1988, 21 cents of every dollar collected came from patient payments. In the next several years, this will be even higher as rising health care costs are shifted more and more to your patients.

Some object to using proration because the computer "can't" do proration, or "it's not accurate." These objections are not valid. Proration can be handled effectively by every major patient accounting system[8] and is the key to effective payment communication, before or after service. It could be argued that proration is the key to an effective admissions, billing and collection process.

The simple truth is that you can't afford not to prorate, and you have to make it work, with or without the computer. Most hospitals don't attempt to use their computer to prorate insurance coverages and patient portion because they feel it's too complicated to establish and maintain.

Phil Morian, an information systems consultant with the Dallas office of Coopers & Lybrand, recently told *Modern Healthcare* most hospitals don't use their automation for proration, even though it is available in their system.

Morian told *Modern Healthcare,* "They could take care of 80 percent of their claims by automating 20 percent of the coverages—the 80/20 rule—but they say, 'Because I can't do all of it, I'm not going to do any of it.' "

[8] Zimmerman & Associates, Inc., *Who's Out There Selling?,* 1992.

IDENTIFY PATIENT'S AMOUNT

The objective of proration is to separate the patient portion from the insurance portion as soon as possible. In many cases, this should be done prior to service. This fairly simple concept has a lot of strings attached to it:

- Computer system capability/utilization
- Quality of insurance company information
- Your pre-admission program
- Are you able to estimate charges prior to service?
- Communicating to the patient

All of the above factors are thrown into making proration work.

One final point. While anyone in the business office can come up with reasons why proration won't work, don't accept their argument. Proration is too important in terms of improved cash flow and patient communication. Put your proration program into place and stick with it until you have the problems worked out.

You can't do much about the increases in uncovered charges and increasing self-pay, but you can do a lot about dealing with it by using proration through your patient accounting system. Self-pay is among your most profitable financial classes. Do everything you can to maximize payment from patients. Start by prorating every inpatient account and start to recognize the patient-pay phenomenon for what it is.

11

You Can Get Assertive Without Messing Up Patient Relations

Many CEOs feel their business office can't be assertive because it will create poor patient relations; the medical staff will get on their back. That's simply not true.

In a recent seminar in Columbus, Ohio, I asked the group, "What's more important—public relations or collections?"

The answer to the question was immediate. "It depends on who's asking the question, but if you're talking about administration, it has got to be public relations," said a group member. But then someone else spoke up and said, "Yes, that's true, but they also want the cash."

There you have it. Cash is king, but public relations is right up there as well.

With increasing deductibles and co-pay, your business office staff will be dealing more and more with your customers. And with competition heating up, you want cash and good patient relations. You want those customers back.

Many CEOs feel their business office employees can't be assertive in their collection effort because it will create poor patient relations, the medical staff will get on their back and they will be fielding complaints all day long. That's simply not true.

But, it doesn't just happen. Assertive collections can take place if planning is applied to the critical issues that cause complaints. The dilemma is to get more assertive *without* messing up your patient relations.

Maintaining favorable public relations while maintaining an assertive collection program doesn't depend *entirely* on favorable face-to-face or telephone contacts by employees.

FOUR FACTORS THAT DETERMINE PATIENT RELATIONS

There are four other factors that determine favorable or unfavorable patient relations. Those include:

1. Collection policy,
2. Collection procedures,
3. Collection practices and
4. Collection notices and letters.

Lack of attention to any one of the above can cause adverse public relations in the collection process, no matter how good your staff's personal human relations.

Here's a review of the above in relationship to maintaining favorable public relations while actively collecting.

1. Collection policy

Develop a collection policy that covers the *majority* of situations and have it reviewed by your administration for approval and backing.

When you don't have a collection policy, your staff will have nothing to fall back on or refer to when a public relations situation comes up. A policy will give you and your staff backing, support and direction.

Develop the collection policy, approve it and then train the staff. Review it with employees from time to time, to be sure it is being followed:

A lack of policy will come back to haunt you and burn you time and again in the collection process.

2. **Collection procedures**

Outdated procedures cause poor public relations. Review the existing collection procedures before and after a public relation problem comes up and question whether that procedure should be revised.

Look at your existing procedures and keep in mind as you develop new ones, *what will this do to our public relations?*

Another aspect of the procedures that cause problems is *the staff did not follow the guidelines* and that's where the problem started. Train the staff in the use of the collection procedures and check often enough to insure they are being followed. Let the staff help develop procedures. In that way, they are more likely to follow them.

Try to keep them from free-lancing, or ad-libbing, and deviating from the procedures—use those creative talents behind the scenes and away from the heat of the moment to plan sound procedures.

3. **Collection practices**

A slightly different aspect that has an effect on collection public relations is the *collection practices* of your staff. This deviates somewhat from policy and procedure.

4. **Collection notices and form letters**

"It's not what you did, but what you *said* and the way you *said* it in your letter!" are comments often heard by the manager. The wording, design and entire image of your collection notices and letters should get close attention in order not to create hostility or confusion leading to a PR problem.

Outpatient services is another area that hospitals often foul up in relationship to patient relations. Outpatient services at hospitals have increased nearly 50 percent over the previous five years according to American Hospital Association's Hospital Panel Survey. With these types of volumes, are you prepared to collect for services at the time services are rendered, without damaging patient relations?

We all can realize the cost effectiveness of collection at the time of service. No additional billing statements or computerized dunning statements would be required. No follow-up telephone calls, and, of course, no dollars tied up in our accounts receivable.

ASK PATIENTS TO PAY AT TIME OF SERVICE

But are we prepared to implement a procedure that most other businesses have long had in place? Can we ask patients to pay at time of service without sacrificing good patient relations? The answer is, "Yes." Here are several tips:

One of the most important steps in this process is to be able to produce a bill when services are performed. How can we expect patients to pay for services if we do not present them with a bill?

You should develop a system, whether computerized or manual, that allows the production of a bill to be presented to patients. Only then can you ask for full payment. To accomplish this task, your fee schedule should be developed to simplify the process. Round off prices to whole dollars, possibly bundle fees for a battery of diagnostic tests.

A second requirement, quite often overlooked, is to make paying for services accessible to patients. Don't ask patients to walk to the other end of your hospital complex to patients to walk to the other end of your hospital complex to pay their bill. Avoid situations where outpatients must stand in long lines with inpatients to see a cashier. Accept and promote use of credit cards.

Educate your patients that payment for outpatient visits is required at time of service. Post notices or signs stating your policy. Educate your medical staff about your policy, because they generate the majority of orders for outpatient diagnostic tests.

Finally, you also must decide to what extent services will be available without payment at time of services. Will all services be provided whether payment is received or not? Should some services be refused?

Decide these policies prior to implementing any policy and set specific guidelines for all staff to follow. Then, ensure that everyone understands and follows these guidelines. Remember, when implementing any policy or procedural changes, there may be some misunderstanding in the beginning. However, in the long run, your business office operation will run more efficiently.

Registration and collection at time of service are the major functions of the registration and admissions department. However, registration without favorable public relations will lead to customer service problems and will collect less in the long run.

Health care is a service-oriented business. Your patients will judge the quality of your facility based on the quality of customer service they receive. All areas of the hospital, from registration through collection, must be prepared to provide superior levels of service to patients.

Most patients know little about clinical medicine, but they do know how they like to be treated. If they are treated poorly during their visit to your facility, do you think they will respond quickly and cooperate with payment? Probably not.

BUILD GOOD PUBLIC RELATIONS

Build public relations into the registration and collection strategy and train everyone on registration techniques consistent with favorable customer service. How well this is done will determine the success of your patient relations. Educating your patients as to what your expectations are regarding their bill and payment go a long way toward maintaining favorable patient relations.

These times call for assertive collecting to improve cash flow. Unfortunately, too many CEOs feel assertiveness can lead to uncomfortable public relations problems.

An in-depth, two-day receivables problem-solving workshop was held by a group of hospital receivables managers to solve those important problems for today's environment. They brainstormed about potential causes of public relation problems in the collection process. Then, the smaller groups of managers came up with recommendations for correcting the situations and, thereby, improving public relations.

As a result, the managers produced an all-encompassing, pro-active public relations program for the entire collection process of a health care provider. Here's their program:

Improving public relations in the collection process

Causes of poor public relations and recommendations

PROBLEM #1:

Poor quality of information from all points of patient registration.

Recommendations:

1. Put registration departments under control of receivables manager.
2. Monitor information and give feedback on errors, omissions, etc. Insist on quality at all points of registration.
3. Stress the importance of getting "more information" at registration.
4. Train registration staff in collection—why information required.
5. Verify critical information with copies of all ID cards, etc.
6. Establish a good, productive pre-admitting program.
7. Use past data on patients. Look it up, and then re-verify.
8. Put more emphasis on pre-admission process.

PROBLEM #2:

Poor quality of bills and collection notices.

Recommendations:

1. Proofread before mailing.
2. Review and rewrite all collection messages and notices.
3. Make all bills easy to read and understand by the public.
4. Reduce late charges.

Continued...

Improving public relations in the collection process—Continued

PROBLEM #3:

Lack of knowledge of what we do in business office by internal departments (administration, nursing, various departments).

Recommendations:

1. Have meetings with various departments to explain our objectives in more detail.
2. Have a regular feature in the organization's newsletter.
3. Have an open house in the business office.
4. Communicate more regularly with administration and other department heads.
5. Invite them to our staff meetings.
6. Make presentations at their meetings.

PROBLEM #4:

Lack of knowledge by the "public" of what to expect from us related to collections and payment.

Recommendations:

1. Do some positive advertising in local newspapers and magazines, and have open houses.
2. Conduct classes for the public.
3. Provide written material to be given at admission and pre-admission.
4. Conduct a public relations survey by telephone after service is rendered to go over charges, bill, collection policy, etc.
5. Use tent cards on patient food trays.
6. Discount bills for immediate payment by the patient.
7. Make personal visits to patient while in-house or more detailed explanation at discharge or after service.

Continued...

Improving public relations in the collection process—Continued

PROBLEM #5:
Poor service by the business office staff

Recommendations:

1. Train the staff—technical items and human relations.
2. Upgrade job requirements.
3. Upgrade salaries and hire better people.

Customer service is a popular topic today. Corporate America says during the 1990s, companies providing excellent customer service will excel over their competitors.

Talking about good customer service and actually providing it is another story. Managers cannot promote customer service on one hand, and then cut salaries, demoralize their staff or foster an unmotivated work force on the other hand.

Retail stores like Nordstrom's, or British Airways, empower their employees to deal with all the needs and desires of their customers. Hospitals need to realize their customers also must be dealt with in this manner. If not, they will lose market share and develop poor customer relations, whether their customers be the patient or the physician.

Here are important points to remember in trying to ensure good customer service:

- Empower your staff to deal with all customer needs.
- Educate the staff on all current developments within the organization.
- Train staff on how to deal with various situations within their area of responsibility.
- Weed out staff that says, "It's not my department," or, "That's company policy—like it or leave it."

- Promote a customer service environment—so when your staff is faced with a customer's problem, they can resolve it. Don't transfer problems to other departments.
- All contacts with customers must promote the organization and its willingness to deal with any of customer request.

Good customer service results in the organization developing patient or physician loyalty which will make a difference in the health care market during this decade.

Don't have the mistaken notion that a more assertive program to improve cash flow and profit form receivables must result in constant and numerous complaints and poor patient relations. It doesn't.

The Total Quality Management approach to improving the quality of patient relations in the billing and collection process works great! So does training and common sense in relation to policy, procedures and the way you communicate to the patient in the billing process—which is the topic of the next chapter, billing the patient.

12

Develop A Bill Patients Can Understand (and Pay)

Patients won't pay what they don't understand. It could be your bills to patients are ineffective because they are confusing.

PATIENTS OFTEN COMPLAIN ABOUT BILLS

How often have you heard your patients complain about their bills? Hospitals are finding that many patients complain they don't understand their bill.

It's no secret—patients won't pay what they don't understand. It could be your bills to patients are ineffective because they are so hard to understand and are confusing.

The Siegel & Gale Perplexity Poll asked 625 adults across the country to rank common forms and documents according to their difficulty and reader satisfaction. On a scale of 0 to 100, medical and dental insurance forms, college financial aid applications and federal and state income tax forms were rated "unacceptable" at 0 to 49, the survey said.

Hospital bills and mortgage applications had a "problem" rating of 50 to 69.

It's probably a good idea to review your bills for clarity and ease of understanding by the patient. Make them simple and easy to comprehend. You want to encourage payment—not confuse the issue and delay payment.

PATIENT PORTION NOT PAID QUICKLY

If hospitals don't take the time and effort to determine and communicate the patients' insurance benefits, self-pay portions of the bill have little chance of getting paid quickly. Most would-be patients have no idea what their deductible or co-pay portions are, and many don't even know what the terms mean.

A recent survey of insured employees throughout the United States showed only 40 percent "completely" understood the term "co-insurance!" Twenty-five percent understood it "somewhat"; 21 percent were "not sure"; and 13 percent had "never heard of it!"

Percent of employees who *do not* understand coverage terminology

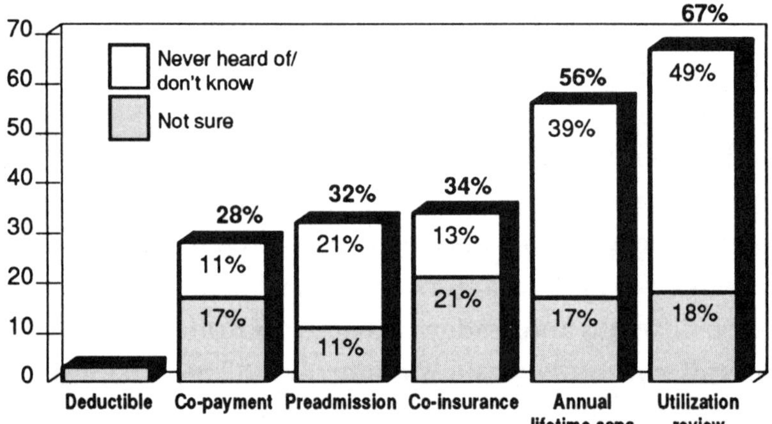

Source: NAPPH, 1991

It's not an inordinate number of errors on hospital bills that cause the misunderstandings and complaints either. For instance, a recent audit of more than 17,000 patients accounts at 28 facilities in four states and the District of Columbia revealed that hospital bills are nearly 98 percent accurate.

Auditors from Chart-Tech Inc., Evanston, Il., analyzed patients' bills during an 18-month period ending in July 1989. They found that the net charge error as a percent of the total charges reviewed was just 2.4 percent.

Of the 17,624 patients' accounts reviewed, the auditors found that 57 percent of those accounts contained undercharges, while 10 percent had overcharges. Also, for every $1 hospitals overcharged, they undercharged $2.25, according to the study.

Here's an advertisement placed in a Sunday paper...

Did your hospital bill make you ill?

Were you confused by your hospital bill?

Do you wonder why Aspirin cost $5.35 or why you had to personally pay for items on the bill?

Hospital bills are in error most of the time and usually in favor of the hospital. BillCheck will screen your bill and let you know whether your bill is reasonable or not. We will tell you what you might be able to do to reduce your cost.

Find out how insurance companies control costs and how you can use these same methods.

Call 123-4567 or 800-123-4567 now for free information.

BILL CHECK, Inc.

Here's the title of an advertisement in *Money Magazine*...

9 Out of 10 Hospital Bills Are Wrong
Here's How to Spot Mistakes and...Get A Refund

Your bills in some ways have always been viewed as "questionable" by your patients, but now it's getting ridiculous. Day after day, the press, employers, insurance companies and patient "advocates" are all attacking the same thing, your bill.

In fact, many patients are convinced that rising health care costs are related to massive overcharging by the health care industry. For example, in the recent *Money Magazine* article, there were two highlighted quotes:

> The typical hospital bill comes to $10,000 and is likely to contain mistakes or overcharges that range from about $500 to $700.
>
> Insist that the hospital staff clearly explains to you any bill that seems complicated or one that is more than, say, $20,000.

The article also goes on to say the most common billing errors are inaccurate charges, duplicate charges and inappropriate charges.

While no one in receivables management will suggest our bills are error free, the idea of intentional overcharging is just plain wrong. Most billing errors are just honest mistakes, but the public is not buying this anymore.

FIX THE BILL

Faced with this situation, you need a new strategy. Here are a few suggestions:

1. **Explain the billing process to your patient before or at time of service.** One reason why your patients are suspicious may be that no one talks to them about their bill. Have a process in place to tell your patient how the billing works—prior to service if possible.

2. **Clean up internally.** Many times bills are wrong. Sloppy charge posting, late or wrong charges are all too common. A good pre-audit program can help you find these errors before your bill is ever sent out.
3. **Train your staff on the telephones.** When your patients call with questions, make sure you're ready for them. If patients get the "runaround" when they call in, it will make the situation worse.
4. **Review your statements/dunning notices.** Many billing complaints are a result of misunderstood statements or dunning notices. Send out communications your patients can understand.

One of the problems is that third-party payers are requiring so much information from providers to process the correct reimbursement. The bill is becoming geared more to the insurers needs than to the patients needs. This results in payment delays due to patient inquiries and more confusion.

Some hospitals are taking steps to alleviate the problem. We interviewed some of these hospitals.

Patricia Arnold, director of patient accounts at the 325-bed Mercy Hospital, Hamilton, Ohio, said, "The hospital has implemented two methods of dealing with billing problems. First, the statement itself contains pre-printed explanations on the back, including phone numbers of the different departments. A direct line to Medicare is also included. Second, the customer service department supervisor has set up quality assurance and follow-up."

"For instance, complaints will be forwarded to the responsible department, (which) must reply in five days. So far, so good," she says. "The problem is when a patient requests a copy of the detailed bill. We then will get an internal auditor. It's time consuming, but keeping patients happy is one of our most important functions." Arnold also point out, "Our credibility has gone up as a result of our efforts."

BILLS CHANGED BASED ON PATIENT POLL

St. Francis Hospital, a 260-bed facility in Milwaukee, undertook a different approach to combat patient complaints. Mollie Diel, director of patient financial services, said St. Francis has modified their bills.

"This was done because of an opinion poll we had done. A majority of people favored changes to our bills," Diel said.

A data mailer is sent to patients which contains the following modifications: added color, such as a payment portion in red; larger-sized print; and sequenced reports.

One of the kickers in this bill dilemma was pointed out by Bob Rademan, vice president of finance at Froedtert Memorial Lutheran Hospital, a 384-bed hospital in Milwaukee. Rademan pointed out to us that "there are incentives for patients to find errors on their bill. Insurers are promising up to a one-half reduction in a patient's bill if they find errors."

The problem is that more and more patients will ask for the detailed bill, resulting in further payment delays, regardless of whether they understand the bill or not.

You might want to do what some hospital CEOs are doing in an attempt to make bills more user-friendly. The hospitals throw the problem back to the business office staff members and ask them to come up with ideas for improving the "patient's understanding and comprehension" of the bill.

Some have come up with ideas to make the bills easier to read and understand. Others have created special brochures answering common billing questions, employing a generic billing statement to provide explanations for the codes and numbers that bills typically contain. Still other hospitals have gone directly to their patients for ideas to reduce billing complaints, and then put their suggestions into affect.

In any case, make the development of a bill patients can understand and pay one of your major projects to improve cash flow and patient relations.

13

Stop the Bad Debt Hemorrhage

Profit and cash needlessly lost due to ineffective receivables management

TOO MUCH BAD DEBT

Asking how bad the bad debt is for hospitals is like asking how bad it hurts when an elephant is standing on your foot. It's extremely painful, but you wonder what you can do about it. And you may not know how bad it is until the elephant lifts its foot!

It's time hospitals got the elephant off their foot to see just how bad the damage is. Believe me, it's bad.

While the nation's hospitals are watching their operating profit margins hover around the low 2 percent mark, they also are witnessing bad debt figures that have become equally staggering and concerning.

It is estimated, based on our projections from the 1992

HARA (Hospital Accounts Receivable Analysis Report), that hospitals could write off $14 billion to bad debt in 1993. Add charity write-off to that number, and you're looking at an uncollectible total that could reach nearly $25 billion. It was less than $3 billion back in 1980. That's an 800 percent increase in 13 years!

Based on conservative projections, the 1994 uncollectible figure could top $30 billion. It is safe to say bad debt is seriously hurting hospitals these days.

Even at your own hospital, your bad debt probably is in the millions of dollars each year and valuable revenue is unnecessarily lost. An average 200-bed hospital in Iowa will write off between $1 million and $2 million to bad debt each year. Double that for the same size hospital in New York, Texas and California.

TWICE AS HIGH AS IT SHOULD BE

In our opinion, the bad debt is about twice as high as it should be. Our experience shows most hospitals pay little attention to collecting self-pay. Efforts to collect self-pay accounts most often are sporadic and ineffective. *As a result, millions are written off each year that should be cash and profit.*

Reducing your bad debt and increasing the dollars collected has a direct impact on operating profit. More so even than improving the days revenue outstanding.

If you reduce your annual bad debt by 50 percent, you can probably get as big a hit to your bottom line as you would by laying off 5 percent of your full-time employees.

For instance, a 200-bed hospital in Iowa with a 1.7 percent operating profit on net revenue of $28 million a year with bad debt at 6 percent of gross revenue dollars would write off $2.2 million to bad debt. Cut that in half by collecting it, and $1.1 million of net dollars goes directly to profit.

Recent developments are causing even a greater negative impact on hospitals. Enough so that we would suggest you may want to take a closer look at your own bad debt write-off.

First is the issue of contractual allowances. As contractual allowances increase (a recent *AHA Monitrend* report shows that hospitals average close to 35 percent of their gross charges in contractual allowances), hospitals are seeing a negative impact on their profit. As contractual allowances increase, the financial classes where you can make a profit decrease.

One of those financial classes where hospital profit can improve is in self-pay. As the HMOs, PPOs, Medicare and Medicaid take a bigger bite through contractual allowances, collection of self-pay takes on added importance. Bad debt makes a direct hit in that profitable financial class.

In tracking your bad debt, you may want to look closer at the percentages. For instance, the traditional percent of bad debt to gross revenue indicator may no longer be valid. A more practical approach to tracking bad debt may be to look at the percent of bad debt to net revenue.

In fact, it may be prudent to look even further at your self-pay in terms of what portion is being written off to bad debt. If contractual allowances are eroding profit, collecting 97 percent to 98 percent of self-pay becomes a standard of excellence for which most hospitals will have to aim.

Secondly, many hospitals try to recoup their bad debt expenses through a variety of techniques. A 1992 court ruling on uncompensated care could change that. A federal court in New Jersey ruled to bar hospitals from increasing rates to recoup Medicare shortfalls and discounts that hospitals give to other benefit plans. It would seem that self-insured groups will fight the shift to recoup bad debt expenses, as will other payers.

WRITE-OFF OVERLOOKED TOO LONG

Bad debt in too many hospitals has been overlooked for too long. It is presently too high in the nation's hospitals, too often overlooked and too important to the bottom line not to receive a closer scrutiny and better results.

Here's one more view of the importance of controlling self-pay that too often is written off to bad debt...on the surface.

When comparing hospital write-off to bad debt to other forms of similar credit, i.e., department stores, retail credit, credit cards, etc., it doesn't look too bad.

Hospitals nationally are averaging 4 percent write-offs of gross charges. Retail credit averages around 4 percent for department stores and 4.5 percent for credit cards.

However, the comparison is a poor one because hospitals should compare the write-off percentage of self-pay revenue only—**not** total gross revenue. The larger percent of hospital charges were covered by insurance. Bad debt is created from the self-pay portion only.

HEAVY WRITE-OFF OF PATIENT-PAY SHOCKING

Therefore, a truer picture of a hospital's success in self-pay collections may be the percent of bad debt percentage to self-pay revenue. That could change the bad debt comparison to retail credit considerably—like night and day. The ineffectiveness of hospitals' ability to collect their patient-pay is shocking.

Based on the most current figures of hospital percent of revenue from self-pay and bad debt write-off—hospitals nationally would be averaging somewhere around 30 percent of self-pay revenue written off to bad debt—a far cry from the 4 to 5 percent of average retail credit.

Statistics from various sources show self-pay to constitute well over 17 percent of total hospital net revenue. Figures from a Zimmerman & Associates Inc. national survey put the hospital bad debt average nationally at approximately 4 percent.

Here is an example of the bad debt to self-pay computation, taking a hospital with $75 million a year in net revenue, a 4 percent write-off to gross revenue and a very conservative 15 percent of revenue from self-pay.

Showing bad debt as percent of self-pay[2]

	Hospital annual net revenue	Self-pay 15% of total net revenue	Bad debt[3]— 4% of total net revenue	Bad debt— % of self-pay
Example	$100 million	$15 million	$4 million	27%

For a more realistic comparison, hospitals may want to compare the write-off as a percentage of self-pay revenue instead of total revenue.

How much of a typical hospital's self-pay winds up in bad debt and charity? Would you believe more than half? Why not? Here's information that appeared in the 1991 Health Care Advisory Board Company report that tries to prove the majority of a hospital's self-pay goes to a collection agency as bad debt or is written off to charity. Read and weep.

It's probably not much different at your hospital. Your business office is more than likely writing off half of the profitable self-pay revenue to bad debt and charity.

[2] Bad debt does not include charity.

[3] See note 2 above.

Advisory board hypothetical shows 57 percent of hospital self-pay written off

Typical hospital annual gross revenues	$102 million[4]
Typical ratio of bad debt and charity to gross revenues	6.0%[5]
Typical bad debt write-off (annually)	$6.12 million
Typical hospital patient pay revenue[6]	$10.71 million
Bad debt and charity as percentage of patient pay revenue	57.0%

Why do some hospitals in the same bed size or community size write off more bad debt than others?

WHY SOME HOSPITALS HAVE HIGHER BAD DEBT

As with everything else, there are some hospitals much worse off and writing off a higher percentage of their gross revenue than others. Comparative hospital statistics between those with a high write-off to those with a lower write-off from our Second Quarter, 1992 *HARA (Hospital Accounts Receivable Analysis)*, indicate some reasons for the differences.

Hospitals with higher bad debt percentages have almost twice as much self-pay revenue, considerably less Medicare and Blue Cross revenue and much more Medicaid. They also have fewer collectors in their business office and spend less on collecting. As a consequence, they have twice as many ac-

[4] Deloitte and Touche and Health Care Investment Analysts, Inc., *The Sourcebook, The Comparative Performance of U.S. Hospitals*, 1989. Average 400-bed hospitals' revenues estimated by assuming average occupancy rate of 73.4 percent, average length of stay of 6.52 days, average gross revenue per adjusted admission of $6,329. "Adjusted admission" includes both outpatient and inpatient revenues, by determining the ratio of gross patient revenues to gross inpatient acute care revenues. Revenue for hospital in market with high managed care penetration may be overstated as utilization, LOS likely lower than national average.

[5] Percentage obtained from Zimmerman & Associates Inc., Hales Corners, Wis.

[6] Assumes contractual allowances of 30 percent, resulting in net revenues of $71,400,000 on gross revenues of $102,000,000. Further assumes that patient pay revenues are 15 percent of net revenues (15 percent is weighted average of the two expert estimates).

counts on the open aged trial balance, and more self-pay in receivables.

Profile of hospital with high bad debt

(Comparing hospitals with 7.1 percent to those with 4 percent)

Hospitals with the higher bad debt have:

- Twice as much self-pay revenue
- 23% less Medicare revenue
- 57% more Medicaid revenue
- Half as many collectors on staff in the business office
- Poor cost-to-collect ratio. Spend far less to collect
- Twice as many open accounts
- Higher percent of self-pay on accounts receivable

However, it is almost as though those hospitals with the odds stacked against them are bent on self-destruction. For instance, those with more self-pay and Medicaid and less Medicare also have half as many collectors and spend less to collect. The poor results in heavy bad debt write-offs become predictable.

In looking beyond the increase in self-pay as reasons for the increase in bad debt, there are other tell-tale signs. The national survey shows the hospital collection department is inexperienced, underpaid and understaffed compared to those hospitals with lower bad debt.

The statistics show the hospitals with higher bad debt have collectors who average two years of experience and have virtually no previous collection experience. Figures also show that the supervisors of these collectors also have little, if any, actual on-the-job collection experience.

Hospital collection departments also are understaffed to handle their present dollar and account volume. Compared to any other collection-to-account volume in other industries, hospital collection units don't have nearly as many collectors. *HARA* also shows that hospitals with the highest write-off to bad debt also have the poorest collector-to-account ratio.

BASIC REASONS FOR THE BAD DEBT BINGE

- Increase in self-pay portion of bills in recent years
- Low salaries—attracting inexperienced collectors and supervisors
- Inexperienced collectors—most have no previous collection experience
- Understaffed collection unit
- Lack of automation in collection process
- Lack formal training. Most collectors have never received formal training in how to collect in hospitals.

With bad debt having a direct impact on profit or loss, hospitals will have to pay more attention to tightening up the entire collection process. A reduction in bad debt can have a positive dollar relationship to the profit margin. Reversing the recent trends in write-offs seems imperative.

CLOSER LOOK AT RELATIONSHIP OF UNINSURED

Because figures in one of our recent surveys indicated regions of the nation with higher uninsured also have higher bad debt, it might be worthwhile to look at the uninsured issue a little closer.

The number of uninsured keeps getting changed. The actual number of uninsured people has also been the subject of debate among researchers and policymakers. A study released in 1990 based on preliminary data from the 1988 Current Population Survey (CPS)—a national survey conducted by the U.S. Bureau of the Census—showed that the number of uninsured is 31 million rather than the 37 million reported in the 1986 and 1987 surveys.

The reported decline (the subject of much controversy among policymakers), was attributed to changes in the 1988 survey form. A 1989 CPS survey, repeating the new methodology, shows 33 million uninsured.

But hold on. Now, there's yet another study that shows the latest number of uninsured Americans is 34.5 million, according to the Employee Benefit Research Institute. This total, based on March 1990 data, is comprised of people who are neither privately insured nor eligible for publicly funded medical care programs.

This report also broke out income earnings for the uninsured. Note that 42 percent of these 34.5 million uninsured earn $20,000 or more a year, and 15 percent earn $40,000 or more.

The study reveals that, contrary to popular belief, the average uninsured American is not unemployed or homeless. Instead, the uninsured American is young, self-employed or working in a small business, and earning at least $20,000 a year. That person is married, a father, and lives in a rural area of the Southwest. (Ten million of the uninsured are children.)

However, it is also interesting to note that half of the individuals with no health insurance obtain coverage within four months, and only 15 percent have uninsured periods lasting longer than 24 months, Urban Institute researchers in Washington, D.C. reported in the fall 1990 issue of *Inquiry*.

Based on responses by some 20,000 adults to periodic Census Bureau questions over a 32-month period starting in 1983, the study also found that people who have jobs in the first month of an uninsured spell are highly likely to have only short periods of no coverage.

What this means is, while a patient may not have coverage

on one visit or stay, they more than likely will the next time. While it may not directly help collect the uncovered charge, it may give you leverage—another reason for close communication between the registration areas and collection unit.

One thing that is clear is that there has been a relationship between bad debt and the number of uninsured. The number of uninsured has and will continue to negatively impact bad debt—unless you take specific steps to offset some of the hit.

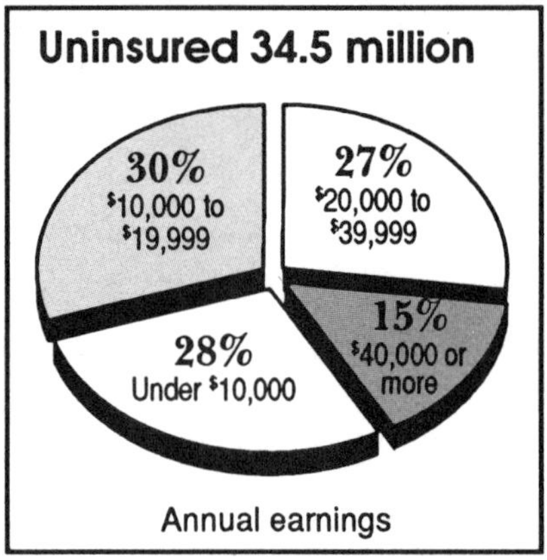

Inforum, a health care planning and marketing firm in Nashville, surveys 100,000 consumers annually on a variety of health care topics, including the prevalence of health insurance. Inforum's *Pulse* survey data on health insurance coverage is household-based and shows the number of households (versus individuals) that are uninsured.

UNINSURED DON'T NEED TO WIND UP BAD DEBT

Your uninsured patients don't need to wind up as bad debt. Almost three-fourths of the estimated 37 million Americans without health insurance are employed. That means most can pay.

Therefore, your business office staff can and should be able to collect the majority of the uninsured accounts. Overall, the ranks of the uninsured grew 1.3 million last year to a record 34.7 million, says a study by Public Citizen, which backs national health insurance.

The latest scientific estimate is that 34,717,000 people

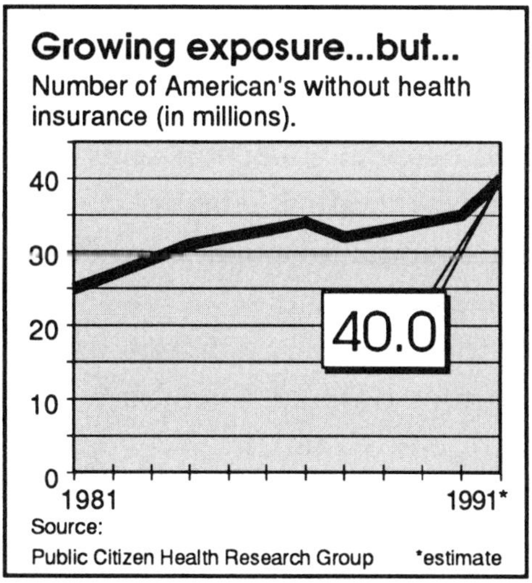

had no health insurance whatsoever in mid-1990—13.6 percent of the U.S. population.

All of this says you should have your business office staff put more emphasis on making financial arrangements prior to a patient's discharge. It's important to note—uninsured doesn't mean the patient lacks the ability to pay. Seventy-five percent of the nation's uninsured are either working or a dependent of someone employed. High write-offs to bad debt connected to uninsured suggests ineffective collection and financial counseling—and should be simple enough to correct with more effective financial counseling and collection activity.

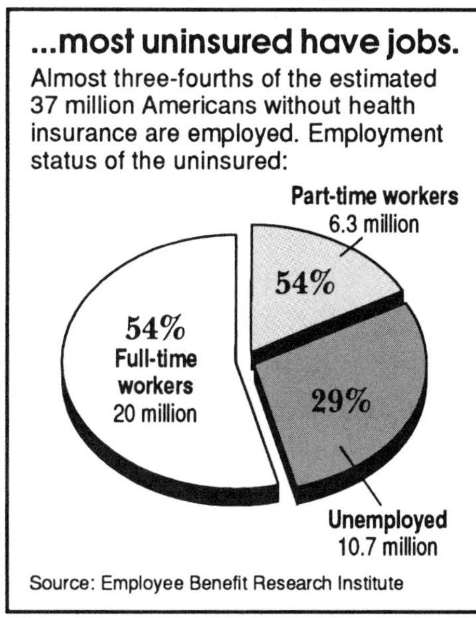

BAD DEBT CAN BE REDUCED

We have performed more than 100 consulting projects during the past seven years. It is very clear to us that hospitals could do a much better job at collecting their self-pay accounts and, thereby, reducing their bad debt.

Most hospitals simply do not do a good job of collecting from the patient. Frankly, most don't pay enough attention to this aspect of improving cash flow and profit. They just don't see the promise it offers. Most hospital collection units are woefully understaffed and under-qualified. The collection staff also lacks automation, direction, and the needed CEO and CFO support to make it happen.

Our suggestion would be for you to focus your attention to this aspect of receivables in your hospital. Encourage the manager to staff it properly with good, experienced collectors who will protect the patient relations aspect and still collect. Get the unit the most up-to-date automated collection system you can find for your situation. Set goals. Track results. Pay bonuses.

As a result, you should see an immediate positive affect on cash flow.

The nation's hospitals' legacy from the past decade is a mountain of bad debt and charity. After receiving the news from the Healthcare Financial Management Association regarding slim operating margins, return on equity and high net days revenue outstanding—the increasing write-offs take on a scary tone.

The logical conclusion is that if hospitals would substantially reduce their bad debt, their financial situation would probably improve dramatically. Good receivables management would result in a lower write-off percentage. Maybe 50 percent less. The correlation is that, if the bad debt percentages improved for the industry, so would the hospital's operating margin.

Look at your own bad debt. How high is it? In my opinion, anything over 2 percent of gross revenue is too high for most hospitals. Only hospitals in the inner-city or public hospitals should be higher.

Has it been climbing at your hospital? Have the dollars and percentages climbed over the past few years? Be careful to review both the dollars and percentages of gross revenue and net revenue.

The percentage of gross revenue could be staying at the same level, while the net dollars have climbed disproportionally higher because of high contractual allowances and greater amounts of patient pay in recent years.

Bad debt at most hospitals has been too high too long. That's also probably true at your hospital. It doesn't have to be. It shouldn't be.

14

Use Banks and Credit Cards to Finance Your Patient-Pay

Convert patient-pay into cash and profit instead of bad debt and long, drawn out installment payments.

REMOVE PATIENT PAYING ON INSTALLMENTS

Many patients try to delay paying their portion of the bill in full. They look to spread their obligation over a period of months or years to minimize their outlay. But, patients paying the hospital on the installment basis just adds to your problem. In fact, it is the problem.

What can be done with the ever-increasing patient-pay receivables that wind up in bad debt instead of profit?

Small monthly payments may not be worth the paper they are printed on. For example, in a recent audit, we identified a patient paying $37.50 per month on an original balance of $9,621. Without interest, this balance would be open for an amazing 22 years.

However, when accounting for lost interest, inflation and billing costs, you would be out $7,096 at the end of the 22 years (assuming your patient would actually pay this long). So in this case, you would actually be better off accepting an original lump sum payment of $2,525.

The value of your money collected months or years after service has far less value than money at time of service. It's also expensive for you to follow up on delinquent slow-pay accounts and small payments. With a recession still staring us in the face, you will want to drastically reduce the number of self-pay accounts paying you on an installment basis.

An aspect of improving cash flow is to get someone else to finance much of your self-pay receivables—letting a financial institution carry accounts that need monthly payments. Ideally, you will want to stay away from contract payments at your organization. They tie up cash, require follow-up and generally are too costly to carry. Charging interest has never been a viable alternative for health care receivables.

So, finding an alternative to handle self-pay accounts that need monthly payments is an ideal way to improve cash flow.

BANK FINANCING PATIENT-PAY ON INSTALLMENTS

Bank financing can provide this alternative. Bank financing is not a new tool to finance self-pay in hospitals, but can be an effective means to control, and even reduce days outstanding.

First, select a local bank that is well-known to your area patients and arrange for a loan program that is easy for both you and your patients to handle. Get a quote on a competitive interest rate that will make it easy for you to sell. Because you will probably endorse all notes with full recourse, it should be easy to persuade the bank to handle the program.

If the patient has a balance and wants to pay monthly, you

can have the patient sign a note. The patient then will make monthly payments to the bank and not to the hospital.

You, in turn, are paid in full by the bank. With this arrangement the monthly payment will fit the patient's budget, the bank is drawing interest on the account and, most important to you, you have money to be put back into use and reduce receivables.

Having the account paid in this manner eliminates the need for additional paperwork for billing and collections, and it is cleared up soon after discharge.

When patients agree to sign a note, you normally fill out a credit application furnished by the bank on which you complete all the patients' credit information. Their address, number of dependents, employer, position, time employed there, monthly income, where they bank, amount of their mortgage and credit references are on the application.

Patients also sign the promissory note at that time for the total of the principal plus interest. The note indicates the amount of the loan, the proceeds, the interest, and the number and amount of monthly installments. The bank remits to you the proceeds of the note.

Usually, the bank will purchase all of your notes without prior credit checking, and no restriction on the terms, other than the maximum length of the contract and minimum to be financed established by the bank—the time of three years. However, these notes are usually subject to full recourse, which means repurchase by the hospital at the default on payments. Our experience shows repurchase by the hospital runs from about 10 percent to 15 percent of the total dollars sent to a bank.

On loans that are not being paid properly, the bank will normally contact the patient by letter and one personal phone call when necessary. The hospital must repurchase the note before it is 90-days past due, or prior to this if the bank deems it uncollectible because of unemployment, bankruptcy, etc.

Some of the nation's more creative banks are taking a closer look at health care's growing self-pay. These banks see a need for the hospitals to rid themselves of carrying accounts on an installment basis, and a way for the banks to make a pretty fair profit.

SOME BANKS GO NATIONAL

Several banks have geared up for a national promotional campaign to hospitals and clinics providing loans to patients with a self-pay balance who want monthly payments. One of these banks is Aetna Bank in Chicago (312-935-6000).

In these programs, the hospital or clinic signs up the patient for the loan and ships the paperwork to the bank. The bank pays off the hospital at once and collects from the patient. If the patient defaults, the hospital must repay the bank.

Recourse with Aetna is set at 60-days delinquent. Providers working with Aetna are averaging around 10 percent buy back so far. The average loan is $1,800. Aetna's interest on the loans—adjustable every six months—is slightly lower than other consumer loans.

St. Francis Medical Center in Monroe, La., became interested in a bank finance program when their up-front financial counseling process was strengthened in late 1991. Hospital executives decided one of the prerequisites of the program was to work with a "hometown bank" to finance their self-pay accounts.

CFO Dee Warlick told us, "My concern with an out-of-state institution was community acceptance. We were asking our patients to think of their hospital bill in a new way—and recommending they consider borrowing the money to pay us. That's a big step. We thought it was essential that our patients be comfortable with the bank."

"Dee did her homework and came in with some pretty detailed specifications on how the program should operate," according to Monroe's First American Bank President, George Campbell. "She was clear on the need to provide St. Francis patients with reduced interest and streamlined approval."

"We were very excited about what we perceived was a win-win arrangement. We sincerely believe that our partnership in this program has benefited the community, the hospital, and represents a terrific business opportunity," Campbell told us.

As we talked to Warlick and Campbell at length, it was clear the program was significantly more than a convenient business arrangement. Included in the agreement were the following:

- Loan documentation is prepared by the hospital and forwarded to the bank for processing.
- Credit application is similar to the format used by credit card companies. However, credit approval is at the hospital's discretion—not the bank's.
- Bank provides specific collection activity throughout the term of the loan and notifies the hospital if the patient defaults.
- Interest rate is below market consumer rates for unsecured loans. Although loan rates are fixed, prevailing rates are negotiated on a regular basis.

Interestingly enough, First American Bank executives think so much of the idea that they have actively marketed the program. They have developed an attractive brochure, and are planning two direct mail marketing campaigns.

"We couldn't be happier with First American's support," Warlick said. "Patient participation and community acceptance has been excellent. Our financial counselors actively sell the program on its benefits—They believe in it and, as a result, so do our patients."

DON'T CARRY SELF-PAY ON INSTALLMENTS

Don't carry self-pay accounts on an installment basis. It ties up your funds and creates too many collection problems for your business office staff.

Instead, give patients several options to pay their bills. Those options may include:

- Payment in full
- Maximum of three monthly payments to pay in full
- Payment in full via credit card, or
- Smaller monthly payments via a bank financing program

Allowing patients to choose from a variety of payment options (all of which benefit the hospital) will maintain their self-esteem and improve public relations.

For patients who require installments to pay their bills, look for ways to arrange for patients to pay someone else, such as a bank, credit card or finance company. The hospital, then, is paid in full while patients chip away at the balance through monthly installments.

Probably your best bet is to follow the same course St. Francis took—talk to your local bank. It could be a win-win situation that needs exploring by both you and your bank.

For a bank loan program to be successful, everyone involved in the collection process (from preadmission to follow-up) must effectively "sell" the patient on using the bank financing program. Here are some tips to help convince patients to use bank financing:

- The credit policy of the hospital must clearly indicate monthly installment arrangements are only administered through the bank financing program.
- If a patient has no credit history, the bank loan will be an opportunity to establish one.

Statistics prove medical bills are on the bottom of patients' priority lists. Bank loans are given better attention. Patients with monthly installment plans through an effective bank financing program are more likely to pay promptly than those paying at the hospital.

A proven way of reducing small balance accounts that may not qualify for a bank note, is promoting credit cards by patients. Patients owing small balances will use credit cards, but you've got to ask them!

PROMOTE USE OF CREDIT CARDS

Here are four ways to promote plastic:

1. Before service or at time of service instruct your cashiers to say, "Your portion of the charges is $100. We accept cash, check, and all major credit cards." You'll be amazed how many of the patients will use the credit card option.
2. After service, make sure your bi-monthly billing statements indicate credit card acceptance. Have a space conspicuously available for credit card numbers.
3. When patients call your office, instruct your business office staff to say, "All major credit cards are accepted. Would you like to put this on your credit card?"
4. Track your department's credit card use. Set monthly goals, and celebrate when you have a good credit card collection month.

As with credit cards, track bank loan activity. Set individual and departmental goals. Promote bank loans as a way to assist your patients who want to make monthly payment arrangements.

15

Analyze Your Payer Mix

Pay close attention to the payer mix of your revenue. It impacts profit, cash, and dictates strategy.

DETERMINE PERCENT OF REVENUE FROM EACH PAYER

One of the areas you want to pay close attention to is the payer mix of your revenue. It has an direct impact on profit, cash flow and internal staffing.

Analyze what percent of your revenue comes from which payer. Consider those payers, like Medicare, Medicaid and managed care, that have contractual allowances eating into your profit. How much commercial, Blue Cross and self-pay (more profitable) revenue do you have?

Seven out of 10 hospitals will lose money caring for Medicare inpatients in 1993, the American Hospital Association reported. Hospitals will pay out $9 billion more than they receive in fiscal year 1993 for Medicare inpatients, the association said; the average shortfall per patient will amount to almost $900.

Your particular hospital payer mix will also determine how much cost shifting will have to take place, and the extent of contractual allowances. Basically, it will spell out profit potential and how hard your employees will have to work to get it.

Cost shifting. The name of the reimbursement game in health care. We all know how it works: The government and HMOs pay less, commercials pay more and some don't pay at all.

But let's take a closer look.

Cost shifting gets major press these days. Hospital cost shifting may be one of the reasons for the large increases in health plan rates, but it also points to your most profitable financial classes. Commercial insurance and self-pay are where the "shift" winds up, according to a book titled, *The Crisis in Health Care: Costs, Choices and Strategies,* co-authored by Richard L. Clarke, president of the Healthcare Financial Management Association, and Dean C. Coddington, David J. Keen and Keith D. Moore, directors of Browne, Bortz & Coddington, Inc., a Denver-based economic research and management consulting firm.

COST SHIFTING LED TO PREMIUM JUMPS

According to the authors, cost shifting, more than any other single factor, has led to the large increases in health plan premiums in recent years. The authors also believe cost shifting is a major culprit behind the large and growing number (estimates range from 31 million to 36 million) of uninsured Americans. They predict, as premiums continue to escalate, the number of underinsured and uninsured will rapidly increase.

If you look at the chart below, only two groups pay more

than full freight: indemnity/self-funded and self-pay. All other groups pay less. In some cases, far less.

The best profit return on your receivables dollar comes from the commercials and self-pay. If this is true, doesn't it make sense to concentrate on collecting those dollars? For most hospitals, commercial insurance and self-pay are the slowest paying payers.

That's because commercial and self-pay collections also require the most work. Simply billing and then waiting for payment won't cut it. Passively waiting for payment from the commercials and self-pay is to self-destruct. The place to start collections from both commercial and self-pay accounts is before, or at time of service. If you start after service, it's already too late.

Slow pay from commercial payers and self-pay is somewhat created by hospitals. All too often, hospital employees are afraid to ask for payment, or even talk about payment, before service. They are trained to think: The patient might get upset; they might go somewhere else.

This is simply not true.

What upsets patients is poor or no communication, not direct communication. So get the patients involved immediately.

Don't allow patients to pay you on an installment basis. Let someone else carry the account. As was documented earlier, self-pay dollars are too valuable to wait for. Put the patient on a bank note plan or credit card program. This simple process can fundamentally improve your entire collection approach.

REIMBURSEMENT ENVIRONMENT GETTING TOUGHER

The reimbursement environment is tough, and getting tougher. Patients don't really care about this. It's your problem. Faced with this, it makes sense to shift your collection approach along with the cost-shift, much the same as the market has shifted our reimbursement.

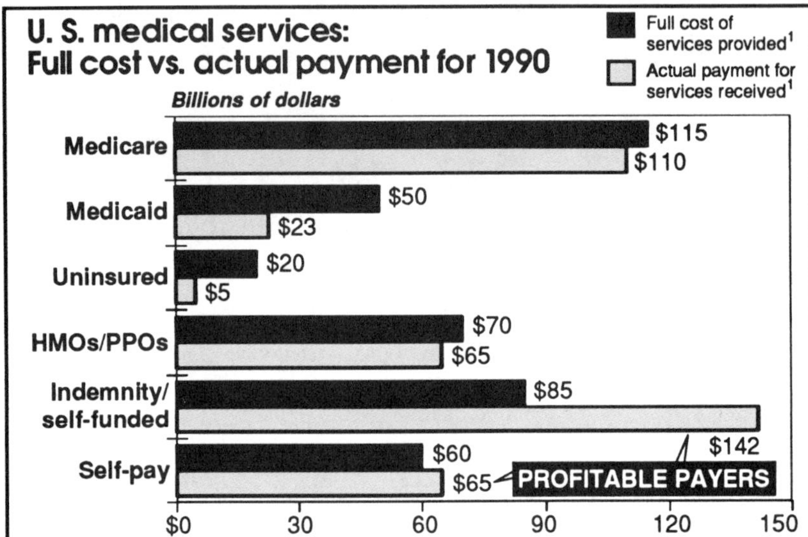

[1] Totals for full cost *and* actual payment equal $400 billion.

Source: *The Crisis in Health Care*, Jossey-Bass Publishers, San Francisco, CA, 1990.

Payer mix also dictates days revenue outstanding. Recent studies show what may be one of the major reasons some hospitals' days revenue outstanding average in the mid-50s and others in the high-90s.

It could basically boil down to how much revenue the hospital generates from Medicare, commercial insurance and self-pay. During the past several years, national surveys show the consistently major statistical difference between hospitals in the 50s and 90s is the payer variables.

For instance, hospitals who average in the high-90s have 76 percent more commercial insurance revenue than hospitals averaging 55 days.

Those with high days also have twice as much self-pay revenue. And finally, those hospitals averaging 98 days have 25 percent less revenue generated from Medicare.

The hospitals averaging in the 50s and 90s consistently show little or no difference in their Blue Cross, Medicaid or HMO revenue. The hospitals also show little difference in staffing or how long it takes to bill the insurance after discharge.

COMMERCIAL AND SELF-PAY SLOWEST PAYERS

It is a proven fact, Medicare is still the *fastest* paying payer hospitals have today. And, at the same time, commercial insurance and self-pay are the *slowest* and *toughest* to collect. Hospitals need a qualified, motivated, well-managed staff that knows what it is doing to successfully collect from those two payer categories.

In my opinion, that's the major reason hospitals with a greater percentage of total revenue coming from self-pay and commercial payers have higher days—quite simply, they aren't collecting effectively from them. Hospitals averaging 98 days also write off almost twice the percentage to bad debt than those in the 50s.

The lesson is this: You need to work more effectively at managing receivables to improve your cash flow and profit picture. Percent of total gross revenue:

- Self-pay, 5 percent or more
- Commercial, 21 percent or more
- Medicare, 36 percent or less.

Our consulting reviews always reveal commercial insurance and self-pay as the two payer groups' hospitals do the poorest job of collecting. Ironically, they are also the two most profitable payers, due to the cost shifting to those categories. Slow pay in self-pay and commercial translates into smaller hospital profits.

Statistical comparisons[2]

	Those averaging...	
	55 GDRO	98 GDRO
Percent YTD gross revenue:		
Self-pay*	3.7	6.5
Medicare	40.2	32.0
Blue Cross	13.0	11.1
Commercial	17.1	26.9
Medicaid	12.1	12.5
HMO	7.0	7.0
Average days from discharge to bill:		
Medicare	12.9	17.4
All other payers	7.9	8.2
Weighted average	9.6	11.0
Percent YTD:		
Bad debt	2.9	4.4
Charity	1.1	2.9
Total uncollectibles	3.9	7.3
Percent discharged receivables:		
Over 90 days	24.2	37.2
Over 120 days	16.3	28.6
Self-pay	10.2	11.6

[2] Not prorated. Self-pay 10 to 15 percent higher than shown here

Source: Zimmerman & Associates Inc., *HARA (Hospital Accounts Receivable Analysis), Third Quarter, 1992.*

Another important factor in your payer mix is the amount of revenue generated from self-insured employers. It seems state-mandated health insurance requirements are actually creating less insurance coverage and indirectly creating more bad debt for hospitals. Watch out for coverage generated from the self-insured employers.

In the past 20 years, there have been mandates passed by states that require insurers to cover either specific diseases or providers, or to make insurance available to individuals who otherwise would have difficulty getting coverage.

Not long ago, some health care benefit gurus were predicting that an ever-increasing number of companies would be rushing to self-fund their health benefits. By assuming the risk for covering employees' health care needs and eliminating the middleman, employers presumably could reap big financial rewards, and avoid the mandated health benefit situation.

Method of funding

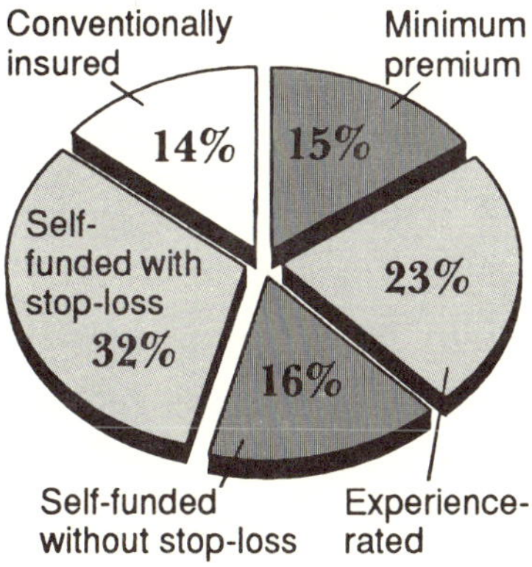

Source: A. Foster Higgins survey, 1988

This year's Foster Higgins survey of 1,962 corporations found that respondents with self-insured medical indemnity plans rose to 59 percent in 1990, compared with 52 percent in 1989.

Some 44 percent of employers with fewer than 1,000 workers were self-insured in 1990, up from 37 percent in 1989. Large employers—those with at least 1,000 employees—also continued the trend toward self-insurance, growing to 73 percent in 1990 from 67 percent the year before.

Health plan options used by employers

	Self-funded employers	Insured employers
Offer HMOs	64	57
Offer PPOs	29	22
Offer 'flex' plans	18	15
Require precertification for elective hospital admissions	70	67

Source: A. Foster Higgins survey, 1988

EMPLOYERS CAN CUT INSURANCE COVERAGE

Also, require your business to watch out for situations on large hospital bills, where the insurance can be suddenly cut or eliminated. A recent court ruling has given most big employers the right to cut or eliminate health benefits when threatened by costly claims.

A federal appeals court held that self-insured employers may alter health insurance policies to sharply reduce benefits for workers who contract expensive illnesses such as AIDS. The 5th Circuit Court of Appeals, in a decision affecting Louisiana, Texas and Mississippi, upheld the right of a Houston music store to slash benefits when it converted to a self-insured plan in 1988. An employee with AIDS saw his lifetime benefits drop from $1 million to $5,000.

Most states have laws prohibiting health insurers from applying such after-the-fact cuts to people who made claims under earlier rules. But when a firm is self-insured, it pays health costs from a company fund rather than paying premiums to an insurer that pays the claims.

Nearly all *Fortune 500* companies and most firms with more than 500 employees are self-insured. Self-insured companies are governed by the federal Employee Retirement Income Security Act of 1974, which exempts them from state insurance laws. ERISA prohibits discrimination against any employee for a claim for benefits.

Track larger bills on self-insured patients closely and hold individuals in the business office accountable for determining the insurance and financial status on a regular basis. Don't get caught "holding the bag" unexpectedly.

When your business office verifies insurance, require them to determine if the patient is covered by his or her employer's self-insurance. It will make a difference in the

The working uninsured

Workers age 18-64 without health insurance

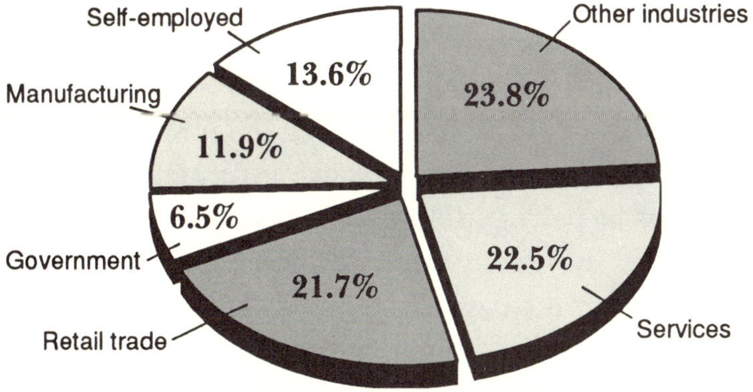

Sources: Employee Benefit Research Institute; Deloitte & Touche

collection follow-up later on, and could alert you to potential collection problems. You may even want to bring this up with the patient when discussing the bill at discharge.

Also, be aware of health insurance companies that aren't what they seem...primarily, solvent! There's a new threat to health care receivables in the form of insurance companies who go belly-up and leave behind a trail of unpaid hospital and clinic bills.

There's a growing number of health insurance providers that organize and act as administrators for groups of small companies. Many are OK. Some are crooks.

SOME INSURANCE COMPANIES ARE CON ARTISTS

Companies that participate in multi-employer welfare arrangements, or MEWAs, as they are called, generally self-insure by depositing premiums in a reserve fund overseen by the administrators. MEWAs, whose premiums are often 10 percent to 40 percent cheaper than coverage from established insurance companies, have caught on; There are at least 3,000 of them.

There are good MEWAs that fill a role. However, be aware there are some that are con artists of the highest degree of cheats. They are ripping off patients and their families in health-related bills that sometimes run into tens of thousands of dollars! Cases are turning up on a regular basis where those con artists sell health policies to small businesses, then siphon off premiums by paying itself big fees instead of building up reserves. They eventually shut down, leaving health care providers holding the bag.

According to the Labor Department which oversees MEWAs, illicit plans have left $300 million to $500 million in unpaid claims. The Labor Department is presently investigating 30 major MEWAs for this kind of fraud.

Unlike insurance companies, MEWAs are not required to register or file any financial papers with most states. So, they have more loopholes to play with, which has attracted unscrupulous operators. Many of them move from state to state when things get a little hot.

What do you do? Well, one thing you might try is to contact the Labor Department's Inspector General's Office and find out who they are investigating—then post the names of those under investigation in your admitting office and business office. Also, you could contact the Insurance Commissioner's Office in your state; they also probably know of the MEWAs who are fraudulent. Don't be a victim of an insurance rip-off.

HEALTH COVERAGE WILL CONTINUE TO SHRINK

The battle over health benefits will rage on in the '90s. A sluggish economy will no longer tolerate increasing health care financial increases without a fight. Hospitals will be the losers in the battle over benefits.

There is growing tension between workers and employers on an issue that is already hot. More than half the workers who struck in the United States last year walked out primarily over their medical coverage. Employers typically wanted to shift some costs of health insurance to employees, and the unions naturally resisted. The unions are going to give in on this one.

Traditional health insurance, the indemnity or fee-for-service plan that lets the doctor or hospital virtually fill in a blank check, costs the average large company $3,200 a year per employee. It went up 21 percent for large firms last year; for smaller companies, 25 percent.

Forecast: Slower commercial and Blue Cross payments to hospitals in the next few years. Self-insured will be more picky about claim audits and create more payment slowdowns.

Managed care will continue to increase. Smaller employers will change carriers frequently, driving your admitting and billing departments crazy with the changes. Look for self-pay to continue to increase with more deductibles and co-pays.

It's not going to get any easier.

16

More Managed Care Means More Cash Problems

Hospitals can't afford to absorb more managed care discounts as cost shifting possibilities dwindle.

DISCOUNTS TAKE THEIR TOLL

Can your hospital survive any more managed care discounts?

A major rule in economics is, you don't sell a product for less than what it costs to manufacture. You won't stay in business long if you do. Yet, isn't this what you are asked to do when you say "yes" to huge discounts as full payments on services provided?

Medicare, Medicaid and Blue Cross plans (to some extent), managed care contracts and various commercial insurance programs, all expect you to accept less. And now, they say there will be a lot more managed care coming down the pike.

Who's left to pay the bills?

Our *HARA (Hospital Accounts Receivable Analysis)* statistics indicate that well over 35 percent of all hospital net revenue comes from the commercial payers and self-pays.

Depending on areas of the country, traditional HMO/PPO products have varied in market share. However, we are now seeing a new managed care product emerge from commercially-sponsored organizations looking to establish provider networks. These networks are promising large volumes of patients using your facility in return for discounts on traditional fees.

Large commercial insurance companies are, at this very moment, developing specific programs to replace their traditional indemnity products to maintain their market share. They are also looking to offset losses in real estate investments, life insurance, and the property and casualty lines. In addition, major employers want to reduce their health benefits expenditures. Insurance companies are hoping hospitals will provide deep discounts to accomplish this.

COST SHIFTING POSSIBILITIES DWINDLE

In the past, you have been able to shift the cost of discounted payers to your commercial and self-pay patients. With a rush toward managed care, more discounts and fewer charge paying patients, how much cost can you shift? This means we need managed care programs that cover their share of the cost. Because you will face more offers to discount your fees, be sure you understand what impact that discount will have. Here are some ideas we can pass on:

- Develop a cost-accounting system allowing you to identify fixed and variable cost by product line.
- Identify how much cost is currently being shifted from existing third-party payers.
- Determine your complete cost for all product lines, includ-

ing fixed costs and those shifted from other payers.

- Evaluate potential loss of pending contracts and the impact on remaining business.

Then, and only then, evaluate if you can afford this new business venture.

Some hospitals are responding more aggressively to these programs. These hospitals are establishing themselves in the marketplace and structuring contracts differently, as opposed to just giving discounts.

- Establish specialty services that will ensure your hospital will be part of all provider networks.
- Select a limited number of product lines and work to improve quality and cost effectiveness. Don't be a "jack of all trades, and master of none."
- Look to negotiate provider contracts directly with area employers.
- Develop a cost-effective environment attractive to the managed care market.
- Develop networks with other hospitals in the area to provide a full-service network.
- Develop networks with your major physician groups to provide a complete product line.

Just offering a discount on services is never a guarantee you will obtain more business and become profitable. Approach all contracts with the data needed to evaluate the financial outcome.

HMOs PULL OFF COUP?

Could it be that HMOs are pulling off a real coup in the health care industry? Are HMOs actually doing all they can to control health care costs? Or are they enjoying the best of both worlds, that is, healthy subscribers and "equal dollars"?

Employers these days are thinking HMOs are getting the better risks from their employees. Older and sicker employees wind up in their non-HMO indemnity plans. According to benefits consultant A. Foster Higgins' *1990 Health Care Benefits Survey: Managed Care,* 59 percent of the 1,955 participating employers thought HMOs were attracting better risks, compared with 53 percent who thought so in 1989.

The survey shows the average cost per employee in HMOs increased 15.7 percent to $2,683. By contrast, medical indemnity plan costs increased 21.6 percent to $3,161 per employee. A major point: Employer skepticism remains high about the ability of HMOs to manage health care costs effectively. The survey shows only 38 percent of the respondents agree that HMOs are effective in controlling costs, while nearly 60 percent believe HMOs are getting the better risks.

However, HMOs say they are the carriers selected because most of the HMOs have no methods for excluding preexisting conditions. And, they say, since their coverage is comprehensive, HMOs are more likely to appeal to larger families, which will increase demand for preventive care.

HMOs get a real boost in their competitive battle with indemnity plans by the federal HMO Act that was passed in 1973. The Act requires companies with 25 or more employees to offer federally qualified HMOs as a health care benefit option. However, this protection for HMOs won't last much longer: The dual-choice provision requiring employers to offer federally qualified HMOs is scheduled to be taken out in 1995. This puts HMOs on a more competitive footing with indemnity plans.

However, the problem of adverse risk selection, along with equal dollars, leaves employers with headaches. As young, healthy employees moved to HMOs because of the fixed fees and broad range of coverage, those employees who remained in traditional indemnity plans usually are older and more frequent users of major health services. As non-HMO costs increase, the premium cost of the indemnity plan increased to reflect the higher use. The "equal dollar" contribution regulation simply meant that any indemnity increase resulted in HMO increases as well.

Insurance companies have become trapped in a "Catch-22". As they raise deductibles and co-payments on the non-HMO plans to control costs, they make their indemnity plans even less profitable. This encouraged even more movement to HMOs.

With almost 59 percent of employers convinced that HMOs get better employee health risks, the burden of proof will be placed on HMOs to prove they are really cost effective. The burden of proof on HMOs will soon increase even more with the 1995 termination date of the dual choice provision of the federal HMO Act.

In my opinion, the only reason HMOs' cost per employee is any lower than the indemnity plans is because of the big discounts they get from providers.

HMO CONTRACT vs. PERFORMANCE

Has your HMO ever shorted you on a payment? It probably happens every time they pay you. As more and more of your business switches to managed care, CFOs need to be ready. Almost every type of managed care contract is different and has a different financial risk.

Managed care products come in three basic packages. Each can require different contract monitoring:

I. Fee-for-service/discounted

This plan pays you a specified percent of charges. Have

your business office track the payments to the negotiated discounts.

II. Per diems

In this case, you can get a uniform rate for each type of service. For example, you may have a different per diem rate for med-surg, ICU or oncology services. The per diem contracts require careful monitoring to make sure you get paid the right amount.

III. Capitation

These contracts get a set amount per member per month. Basically, the provider and insurance company share the risk. Capitated contracts can be difficult to monitor because the fixed payments may show little relationship to the actual services provided.

Because the managed care contracts require so much follow-up, many RMs are using sophisticated software programs. They monitor insurance company compliance to the agreed-upon contracts.

If your revenue mix is more than 10 percent HMO/PPO, you should consider buying a good managed care software product. The costs of implementation will be met in a short time as you hold the HMO/PPO to their contractual benefits. In the long run, you'll come out way ahead.

Finally, if you think the managed care companies are playing hard ball with you now on negotiating discounts—hang on. It's going to get tougher.

We predict that, in the next two years, more and more of the larger managed care companies will acquire many of the smaller, undercapitalized health maintenance organizations. The big guys play rougher and come from a stronger position than you will.

More than 70 percent of all HMO enrollees are in

prepaid health plans with operations in more than one state. That means nearly 39 million people are enrolled in the three dozen health plans that provide insurance across state lines. The number is expected to continue rising, says Inter-Study, a managed-care research group in Excelsior, Minn.

17

Staff with Quality Employees

Competent receivables manager key to success in maximizing cash and profit

GOOD MANAGER WORTH MILLIONS TO BOTTOM LINE

In terms of which hot button a senior executive pushes first to start marked cash and profit improvement from receivables, maybe this should have been one of the earlier chapters; because the selection and nurturing of a good manager of your receivables is certainly one of the most important factors.

In fact, if the receivables manager is truly good enough, you probably don't need to be reading this book.

What's a good receivables manager worth to your hospital? Some consultants estimate a good manager could mean millions of dollars to your bottom line. We agree.

In our consulting and research for books, we have seen enough evidence of what a successful manager, in charge of the receivables, can mean to a hospital. We have file drawers full of case studies where these middle managers have made a substantial impact on the financial position of the hospital.

While researching for the book *Turnaround,* I interviewed dozens of successful receivables managers. You may be interested in what I found in the way of common threads in these successful managers—their common characteristics, traits, their management style, background and approach.

DESIRE TO EXCEL

Their management style or philosophy had a great deal of commonality. There is one clear message that has come from every successful manager I have ever interviewed and studied, and that is—*they all have this insatiable desire to excel!*

In each and every situation, I found these successful managers have a gnawing hunger to be good, if not great, at their profession. They wanted, needed success. So much so, they were willing to make the sacrifices necessary to make success a reality.

In addition, they all could define success. They could see it, touch it, feel it, and point to it. They could show the people they managed that vision of success. They somehow drove their team toward success.

They made winners out of losers, or they dumped them on the wayside. They displayed no tolerance for a losing attitude. Those employees who would not adapt to a winning attitude were cast aside.

I interviewed each of the successful "turnaround" managers, their bosses and their employees. After going through all my notes and taped conversations, I've highlighted the employees' and bosses' descriptions of the managers. Here is a brief capsule of those descriptions:

1. **Successful experiences in their background.** Not all work-related and not all receivables related, but successful.
2. **Courageous.** Tough, firm, persistent. Hold their people accountable.
3. **Leaders.** Motivate and very highly self-confident. Display enthusiasm.
4. **Results oriented.** Focused problem-solvers. They attack, attack, attack, and retreat only to reposition, never to give up or give in.
5. **Communicators.** Turn their people on with their messages. Sell bosses and their people on moving ahead. Provide lots of feedback to their staff. Good listeners.

However, even if you have a good receivables manager, in our opinion, this position is too often underpaid and underutilized.

We think the person in charge of hospital receivables is underpaid. As a result, the position normally does not retain top-flight people. The average director of receivables' mid-point salary range in 1992 is under $47,000 per year. The average CFO is twice that. I think that's too big a difference. CFOs are not overpaid. Manager positions of receivables are underpaid.

It's also our opinion that those in charge of receivables are too often not considered an important part of the hospital management team. Our consulting assignments, seminars and national surveys confirm that CFOs and receivable managers are too frequently not on the same wavelength. RMs, almost en masse, say their position is not recognized for the importance they feel it deserves. They cite example after example of CEOs and CFOs displaying a lack of recognition of their position as receivables managers. In short, the position is often underutilized by the CFO.

MISSING OUT ON OPPORTUNITY

Are CFOs missing out on an opportunity to improve the condition of their receivables by underpaying and not recognizing the importance of this key position in today's hospital cash flow crunch?

We think so.

Our suggestion to CFOs is to up the pay scale (closer to the $60,000 to $80,000 range for hospitals more than 150 beds) and hire the best, most qualified person you can find. Then, treat this person as though he or she is one of the most important department heads in the hospital and hold them accountable for results.

If you're already headed in that direction, great. You'll see the dividends soon enough. If you're not heading that way and you're not happy with the condition of your receivables, you may want to start by upgrading the pay scale of the receivables manager, and then placing the best person you can in the position.

Once that person is on deck, treat them as an intimate part of the management team.

This may be the best single piece of advice I can give you to improve cash flow. I feel strongly that people make it happen—not computer systems, bonus plans, the newest software, state-of-the-art equipment or even consultants. These are all important tools and adjuncts, but it's people that make the difference.

If there's one thing that came out loud and clear from my interviews and research over the past 10 years, it's that human resources is the most important ingredient to success in managing cash flow in hospitals.

Next to the selection of the right manager of receivables, the staffing of your collection unit in the business office is most critical. In the middle of this situation of requiring an improved turnaround from billing to payment and favorable public relations, sits your employees who function as the "collectors." They make a sizable contribution to the financial success and public relations of the organization.

UNDERQUALIFIED, UNDERPAID, UNDERSTAFFED

However, too often these collector positions in hospitals are underqualified, underpaid and there are not enough of them to get the job done. Few of these employees have had collection experience at a bank, finance company or similar consumer credit company. Too frequently, they simply don't know how to collect.

Hospital collectors often set up financial arrangements that prolong payments, rather than take the steps to accelerate the turnaround of the hospital receivables. Without a good collection background in some kind of for-profit company, these collectors become easy prey for clever debtors and slow-paying insurance companies.

Collectors in hospitals are woefully underpaid and inexperienced compared to their peers in banks, finance companies, retail stores and collection agencies. The average hospital collector's salary has increased little in the past two years, according to the *HARA (Hospital Accounts Receivable Analysis).*

Hospital collectors averaged just under $19,000 in 1992. It was $17,000 two years ago. These salaries do not attract the best. The best go and stay elsewhere.

Collector bonuses are almost unheard of in hospitals, while quite common in other organizations dealing in consumer collections. Only hospitals over 400 beds are more likely to pay a collector bonus. The *HARA* report shows 13 percent of the 400-plus bed hospitals pay a collector bonus. Bed sizes from 200 to 400 show 7 percent pay a collector bonus. Hospitals under 200 beds show no listing of paying for performance to collectors.

Most hospitals with their gross days revenue outstanding over 90 have one full-time equivalent collector for every 6,700 open accounts. Hospitals under 50 gross days revenue outstanding have a much better ratio—one FTE for every 3,700 open accounts. Study after study shows one glaring trend. Hospitals with more collectors collect more money and have lower gross days revenue outstanding, as well as a lower write-off to bad debt.

With the increase in patient-pay portions because of changes in the way insurance is paying today, hospitals are getting buried in self-pay accounts. Having enough well-paid, efficient collectors was always important, but now they are indispensable.

Developing a collection staff that has a good FTE-to-open-account ratio with a decent pay scale has become of paramount importance to receivables managers.

Is your business office understaffed? Or is it, by some "accident," overstaffed? Who knows for sure? We have few industry standards to go by. Staffing in hospital business offices has been a disturbing question for years. However, some new data may begin to shed some light on the subject.

A new national survey[1] of hospital business offices has revealed some interesting "averages." The average staffing for hospitals of all sizes breaks out as follows:

- One FTE for every 13.25 licensed beds
- One FTE for every 967 open accounts on the aged trial balance

For the purpose of this survey and consistency of data,

[4] Zimmerman & Associates, Inc., *HARA (Hospital Accounts Receivable Analysis)*, First Quarter, 1992.

hospitals were requested to include staff performing the following functions: insurance billing, insurance verification, patient representatives, cashiers and cash application, refunds and collections. Also included were all managers, directors, or supervisors involved in the above areas. Hospitals were asked to exclude: utilization review and coding staff, precertification staff, and staff involved in the registration functions.

Tip #1:

Check your business office staffing ratios compared to the nation's averages by:

a. Your FTE to your licensed beds, and

b. FTE to number of open accounts on your accounts receivable. You should fall between the norm in "a" and "b", or it may indicate you're under- or overstaffed.

Tip #2:

Just as important as how many employees you have, is to ask yourself these questions—"Do I have them in the right positions?" and "Do I have the right people?"

Quality of the employees within the receivables department is perhaps more important than how *many* you have.

I would rather have fewer more productive, highly motivated, highly skilled employees than more unmotivated, unskilled, less productive employees.

The point here is, if you go through "a" and "b" above and find you are about average in staffing and your receivables are still in bad shape, you probably need to take tip No. 2 more seriously and take a good hard look at the quality of your staff. It's probably not numbers, but quality.

18

Cultivate a Motivational Climate

Employee desire to excel may contribute as much as 80 percent of success in managing receivables.

CEOs AND CFOs TRIGGER MOTIVATION

Managing successfully in hospitals requires specific knowledge, experience and skill. However, what I have discovered when interviewing successful managers for two of my recent books, is that *motivation* plays an extremely important role in obtaining desired results.

Motivation is more difficult for some hospital CFOs to appreciate because it's more of an intangible. They feel motivation is not as easy to get their arms around, to hold, to total up or review as a statistic.

Nevertheless, our many interviews for the books and newsletters show that successful hospital financial executives say motivation contributed to more than 80 percent of their success! Too often, when we see the word "motivation," we think of managers motivating their staff. However, we discovered repeatedly that motivation first starts within the top managers—the CEO and CFO—that if bosses aren't turned on themselves, they won't be practicing motivation effectively with their staff. Instead, bosses will be half-heartedly applying textbook techniques or the latest management gimmicks that never quite brings the promised results.

So, our contention is that motivation of others starts with *you* being motivated!

OFTEN DEMOTIVATED GROUP

Too often we find hospital business offices employ a demotivated, demoralized, downcast group. They often fit the description of being the most "unloved and unappreciated" employees of the hospital. They don't sense their importance in the overall scheme of things.

Some of that comes from the lack of motivation from the CFO or CEO, and some comes from the pure lack of support for the staff in the business office and admitting.

The overriding theme and message we get from business office staff members is they get in trouble when asking for money. They often feel they don't have management and administrative support when they ask for payment in full, deposits, down payments, use of credit cards, etc.

While we find this common among hospital financial counselors, cashiers and admitting employees, managers also tell us the same thing. Support is a special issue for financial managers in hospitals. Financial decisions are sometimes tough to make in the delivery of health care. In my opinion, too often CEOs don't back up a businesslike approach to managing receivables. Frequently, I think, CFOs see the management of receivables strictly as a number-crunching process and ignore the people. Most other departments in the hospital have a tendency to look down on the financial people as some kind of necessary evil—particularly those people who bill and collect for charges.

However, it was a different story for those hospitals I featured in my book, *Turnaround.* We saw boards of directors taking tough stands to support a solid, businesslike approach in hospitals that had previously been giving away the store. We witnessed CEOs who backed their CFOs time and again when the CEOs thought the CFOs were doing the right thing. The CEOs withstood the barrage from physicians who balked at changes and threatened that they would "take their patients somewhere else" if the hospital continued to ask "their" patients for money.

There was evidence the CFOs supported their receivables managers against the irrational tirades of patients, physicians, nursing service, and even the media. I strongly feel support will become a synonym for survival in this business.

Successful fiscal management will not be accomplished by some lone ranger-type catalyst—as important as that one person is in the scheme of things. It will be accomplished when the entire hospital lends support to the project—from board members through the CEO, CFO and those managing the receivables, as well as all of the ancillary departments in the hospital. Anything short of full support throughout the turnaround will seriously cripple cash flow.

CFO/RM SUPPORT TIPS

CFOs can build teamwork with receivables managers with these tips:

- **Goal setting.** The CFO and RM should set receivable goals together; i.e., days, bad debt, budget, etc.

- **Develop action plans.** Again, do it together. How are we going to achieve the goals we set? What's our road map?
- **Monthly report/review.** CFO and RM should review progress monthly, then adjust, correct and stay on course.
- **Track critical factors.** CFO should only review most critical indicators with RM. No need to get "nit-picky."
- **Reward good performances.** CFO should determine some way to reward the good performance of the RM.
- **Celebrate victories.** The CFO should make as many of these "victory" celebrations as possible.
- **MBWA (Manage By Walking Around).** The CFO should drop in on the receivables staff from time to time—just to visit.
- **Go to bat for RM.** RMs need the CFO to break down some doors, or back them up from time to time.
- **Empower and motivate.** CFO needs to know what will empower and motivate the RM to achieve success.

Finally, I came across a meaningful support story from an attendee at one of my seminars:

When a hospital receivables manager says a bad debt figure of a low 1.2 percent is, to a great deal, attributed to the CEO and the support given to business office, you have an unusual story! More often, the opposite is heard from RMs. In this case, Marlene Guerin, business office manager at Northern Michigan Hospital, a 300-bed facility in Petosky, Mich., attributes much of her success in maintaining a low write-off to bad debt to her boss, Jim Raney, the CEO.

"He always gets our side of the story on patient complaints, supports our rather stiff collection policy, and won't back down if we're right," Guerin told me. "We've been together for a long time and we're a team (the CEO and business office) on the collection of accounts."

Financially successful hospitals thrive on support and feed off of it. It is a way of charging everyone's battery and adding an intangible phenomenon that breeds confidence and courage of convictions. This is exactly what hospitals in trouble lack and successful hospitals generate.

TQM PROGRAMS HELP MOTIVATE

As hospitals turn to empowered employees and team-based Total Quality Management programs to overcome productivity, quality and cost problems, many middle managers in the finance divisions are losing their jobs. The executive search segment of our consulting practice reflects that very clearly.

While patients get better service, and front-line workers get greater autonomy and rewards, middle managers wonder, "What's in it for me?" When employees make more decisions for themselves, middle management fears that its authority is threatened.

Those middle managers who are able to hold on to their jobs will find their role in the hospital greatly changed. Many of them have reached middle age and achieved a degree of recognition within their careers and their hospital. Their whole self-image is often based on giving orders, monitoring the work of others and evaluating the final product.

However, it's becoming a new ball game.

According to John Zenger, president of Zenger-Miller, San Jose, Calif., in an article on *Reward & Recognition,* middle managers will need retraining at seminars and conferences to learn to coach, facilitate, ask questions rather then supply answers, and let employees solve problems rather than solving everything for them.

Here's Zenger's advice on motivating your middle managers:

1. **Include them in goal setting and strategic planning for team building.** To create a feeling of ownership in the team program, middle managers should be included in its design from the very beginning. Top and middle management should work together to develop an agreed-upon time line for implementing various tasks that relate to providing excellent service or improving performance.
2. **Reward middle managers on basis of contribution.** Linda Goldzimmer, president of the Linda Goldzimmer Consulting Group, Melville, N.Y., recommends another method to create a feeling of equal ownership in team programs. Reward employees *and* middle managers on the basis of contributions, not predetermined status in the hospital.

   "Middle managers will still be compensated with their annual salary, whether they're participating in the team or not," she says. "As a team member, however, they should share in the same reward as the team, apart from any usual salary compensation."
3. **Encourage middle managers to support teamwork.** Once team programs are in place, they won't grow without support, and middle managers can become an integral part of that reinforcement process. They can help make the program more real to employees. They can work with their groups, or several groups, in the role of coach, and facilitate performance.
4. **Encourage middle managers to self-develop.** Finally, hospitals should back up those skills with training so that managers feel not only competent, but confident to perform.

Middle managers may find it difficult to grow accustomed to the new rules and roles of corporate organization, but, as Zenger points out, they must accept the reality of the situation. "It doesn't matter that they don't like it," he says.

"That's just the way it is."

"In the past, managers believed there was a limited supply of power—if they gave employees power, they had less," he continues. "*Today, they need to learn that the more they empower their fellow employees, the more power they'll have. They must be convinced that they're not competing with employees—they're allies.*"

19

Pay for Performance

Paying for superior performance develops motivational climate. It works wonders for receivable managers and their staffs' performance levels.

SET UP BONUS PLAN

One of the less subtle ways to develop a motivational climate is to set up a pay-for-performance or bonus plan for the employees. It works particularly well for hospital receivable managers and their staff.

Since most of them are not well paid, the extra money has real meaning. And since practically everything they are supposed to accomplish can be tracked and measured, a bonus plan for receivables managers is relatively easy to administer.

Finally—and most important—it will motivate them to achieve high performance, thereby having a direct impact on hospital cash flow and profit.

You probably want advice from someone who has experience developing bonus plans, and I have a few suggestions when setting one up for the receivables manager.

Set it up so that if objectives are met, the bonus is *at least 15 percent of their annual salary*. Also, use net days outstanding, bad debt and percent of aging of the receivables over 90 days as part of the objectives with the highest value. This will help assure they stay focused on the major areas that will impact cash flow and profit.

Also, fit customer relations in there somewhere, if you can figure out a way to measure it.

BONUS PLAN POINTERS

Here are 10 more pointers to use in developing your incentive program:

1. First, have in place a competitive salary structure and a performance appraisal and goal-setting process. Unless employees are paid competitively and are accustomed to working with predetermined goals, they will not accept an incentive plan.
2. Identify incentive targets based on the receivables department's mission and strategic plan. Focus on implementation strategies that require an employee's "extraordinary effort or stretch."
3. Make targets reasonable, attainable and as specific as possible.
4. To avoid any negative impact on quality of care, build strict administrative controls into the plan and base some incentive targets on quality improvements, rather than on bottom-line results.
5. Make sure the plan rewards both teamwork and individual achievements. The correct balance depends on whether the organization's culture and goals lean toward collabora-

tion and "team-building," or entrepreneurship and risk-taking.

6. Base eligibility for the plan on incentive targets that have been identified.
7. Clarify who will administer the plan: the CFO alone, or the CFO with the CEO's input.
8. Ensure that a specific net income level will be reached before any payments are made.
9. Inform eligible employees of all aspects of the plan, including the downside—the various reasons why individual employees may not receive an award.
10. Keep in mind that even the best incentive plan doesn't cure management problems. It won't make incompetent staff members effective or substitute for a manager's strong leadership skills.

Do merit increases (annual raises) motivate stronger performance, or work as an adequate reward for performance given? According to Ira Kay, senior vice president and managing director of compensation consulting for the Hay Group, an increasing number of companies are realizing the limitations of the traditional merit increase many employees have grown to expect.

What's a good alternative? Kay says more organizations than ever are offering employees a base salary and a bonus opportunity. Sharing risks with employees is the wave of the future—a key factor in keeping fixed costs down while motivating employees to stronger performance.

In addition to the receivables manager getting on a pay-for-performance plan, I would recommend developing one for the rest of the business office employees as well.

The key to keeping people motivated through incentives is to keep changing the incentives. What motivates someone now may lose its appeal as time goes by.

INCENTIVE PLANS TO TRY

Here are a few innovative incentive programs you might want to try. Well-timed surprises or individually-tailored perks can do a lot to inspire collectors or everyone in the business office. These four bonus plans could motivate the staff in a variety of ways.

1. **Individual reward plan**

   Plan design: Each month collectors are ranked based on total dollars collected in their area of accountability. The best collector receives a $500 bonus. The runner-up receives $100. This plan motivates collectors individually in the business office.

2. **Team building plan**

   Plan design: Everyone in the business office is eligible, based on the monthly collection totals. The size of the bonus is determined by the monthly collection total.

   The monthly collector goal is obtained from the percent of net revenue collected.

   100% of goal............. $50 per employee
   101-105% of goal.... $100 per employee
   106% and over .... $150 per employee

   This plan puts a premium on team building. If everyone works together, they can get a bigger bonus.

3. **Let's have a party**

   Plan design: Business office throws a "victory party" for the business office and registration staff after a great collection month.

   For some business office employees, recognition is more important than real dollars. This is particularly true if your facility pays well.

4. Merchandise pay-off

Plan design: Collectors are given a monthly quota for cash collections. For each month that collectors meet their goal, they are given a gift certificate worth $100 from a local department store.

These types of rewards may even get their families involved. Family members may put pressure on collectors to hit the goal so they can pick something out at the department store.

Try a different approach. One health care facility recognized topping weekly collection goals with a group announcement and dinner for two at a fine restaurant. It worked for a while, but as more and more people earned them, the dinners lost their impact.

A lottery system was substituted. Employees who topped their goals became eligible for a drawing. Every month, one person's name was picked from a bowl and that person received a $100 bonus.

The new system rekindled enthusiasm, but, in time, it, too, will lose potency. To keep enthusiasm high, ask for reward suggestions from the participants.

There has been a rapid increase in the number of hospitals that have adopted incentive compensation arrangements in the financial departments. Even non-profit hospitals may offer incentive compensation, though such arrangements must be structured carefully to avoid risk to the hospital's tax-exempt status.

Non-profit hospitals can be at risk of losing tax-exempt status when they provide for the endowment of a person or persons above what is deemed reasonable. This is an extremely gray area and is subject to interpretation by the Internal Revenue Service. Incentive compensation packages that are viewed excessive by the IRS can be used as grounds to revoke tax exempt status.

One hospital I know about had similar problems with the administrator's salary. For certain years, Medicare auditors deemed his salary to be excessive and required it to be removed from allowable expenses on their cost report. This resulted in lost reimbursement and was an issue the hospital appealed. The IRS, however, never made an issue of the salary, so tax-exempt status was never in jeopardy.

20

Provide Focus

Use goal setting to keep staff focused on the activities that bring the desired results.

INVOLVE EMPLOYEES

The project of improving cash flow should include involving all of your business office staff members in goal setting, which will keep them focused on the activities that bring the desired results. It will develop teamwork, improve staff morale and increase everyone's motivation. Best of all, your business office staff can produce results in lower days revenue outstanding and bad debt, with proper leadership by the CFO.

When I was with St. Mary's Hospital of Milwaukee, goal setting for myself, and then later with my hospital business office and admitting staff, was, in my mind, the single most important factor in reducing our average days revenue outstanding by more than 20 days—from the mid-60s to the mid-

40s in less than a year—and keeping the days that low for many years.

Then, some years later, when I operated the collection agency as a wholly-owned subsidiary of the hospital and became one of the state's largest agencies in less than three years, goal setting was a major factor in our growth. Now, we always develop a goal setting process when consulting with hospital clients and see it work successfully on a much larger scale.

To be successful, financial departments (which means the people in them) must think success. They must have a *common goal* for which they all are striving. They must take *pride in the excellence* of their work. It becomes an *attitude* toward work.

I believe your attitude towards your job governs not only your own progress, but affects the attitudes and progress of every one of your staff members. In turn, it affects the entire department.

CFOs CAN DEVELOP MOTIVATIONAL CLIMATE

However, CFOs can't motivate their workers. The CFO's job is to ensure that the *working environment enables workers to motivate themselves.*

Goal setting, done individually and as a group in the department, is a guide to how to do just that—develop a motivational climate where the employee becomes self-motivated.

Success is a common goal for normal employees. Author Eugene Jennings is more emphatic, however. He refers to the drive for success as the "success ethic" and says it is self-fueling. That is, the more you get, the more you want. Small wonder then that people call success a *bitch goddess.*

So, setting meaningful goals and achieving them, creates self-motivation—yours and your staff's. And motivation is what makes the cash register ring.

Goal setting and managing by objectives go together for CFOs because they help set the scene and identify where the goals should be set in terms of *importance.* It provides *focus.*

Managing by objectives is a form of management that lives with a commitment—objectives are set and then management takes place around them—organizing, forecasting, planning, control communication and you measure a person's effectiveness by results.

The goal setting process (done with your subordinates)

First:

Development of **Key Result Areas** (the components of your job and that of your subordinate that are most important).

Second:

Develop **Performance Indicators** (these will be indicators of how you will measure your performance in the key result areas).

Third:

Determine the present **level of performance** in the indicators you chose above.

Fourth:

Setting **goals** on the indicators.

Fifth:

Developing an **Action Plan** (the road map that will tell you how you will accomplish the goals).

It's good to have days revenue outstanding as a goal, but you may want to focus on cash collections more than you have in the past. Some CFOs have found that setting goals only on days outstanding too often results in a variety of things happening to lower days—like bad debt and charity increasing, or special discounts for insurance companies in payment. In other words, reduction in days did not always correspond with the same level of improvement in cash.

First, determine your goal in days revenue outstanding, and then the goal in cash collections you'll need to accomplish the days goal.

The following is a hypothetical scenario of a hospital determining goals and its collection standards.

Let's assume you were to take each of your major financial categories within your receivables and develop goals in your total days outstanding. This is the formula you might choose.

ACCOUNTS RECEIVABLE GOALS

Commercial insurance

Present outstanding	Goal	Amount to reduce
$324,000	$224,000	$100,000

If you billed an average of $60,000 a week during the past two months, the present outstanding would reflect five and a half weeks average billing outstanding in commercial. The goals of $224,000 would reflect about three and a half weeks billing outstanding. If you are to gain ground and hit your goal in commercial, you naturally have to collect more than you bill over the next several months. Therefore, you set a goal guideline:

Ratio of collections to billings

Average billing per week	Average collection goal per week	Gain in one month
$60,000	$65,000	$20,000

Conclusion: Adjust collection goals in commercial to $65,000 a week to hit your goal of reduction of $100,000 within five months.

Self-pay (Patient liability)

Present outstanding	Goal	Amount to reduce
$148,000	$100,000	$48,000

You average $15,000 of billing into patient liability a week over the last two months—including outpatient and insurance rejections. Present outstanding reflects **approximately 10 weeks of billing.** The goal of $100,000 would reflect **about six weeks worth** of outstanding in patient liability. Your goals could be set up as such.

Patient liability billing-to-collection ratio

Average billing per week	Average collections per week	Gain in one month
$15,000	$20,000	$20,000

Conclusion: Adjust collection standard in patient liability to $20,000 a week in collections until receivables are lowered and reach an aging of $100,000. Then you can readjust collection standards to equal billings from thereon if you want to stay at that $100,000 figure.

Blue Cross

Present outstanding	Goal	Amount to reduce
$205,000	$160,000	$45,000

Based on the last two month averages, present balance reflects approximately five weeks of bills. Adjust your collection standards to exceed billings by at least $5,000 a week to reach desired goal within two and a half months.

Determining your goal in days revenue outstanding off

this formula might be based on another hypothetical case. First, determine your **average weekly billings** over the **past two months** in each of your categories. For instance:

Average weekly billings

Self-pay	$20,000
Commercial	65,000
Medicare	60,000
Title 19	20,000
Blue Cross	60,000
Miscellaneous	34,000

Then, determine what you feel is a reasonable length of turnaround time you should carry in each category.

For instance, suppose you felt Blue Cross should be turning around in three weeks from date of billing. Then your goal, or standard, to carry in Blue Cross would be three weeks of billing—or three times $60,000, or a total of $180,000 outstanding. Here is a summary of category goals you might arrive at:

Discharged accounts receivable standards to carry

Self-pay		=	$200,000
Commercial	5 wks. x $65,000	=	$325,000
Medicare	3 wks. x $60,000	=	$180,000
Title 19	2 mos. x 20% misc.	=	$160,000
Welfare		=	$30,000
Miscellaneous	3 wks. x $34,000	=	$102,000
Blue Cross	3 wks. x $60,000	=	$180,000

Goals in Total DAR = $1,200,000

In-audit standards or goals

Figure this category by taking the average daily revenue for this month times three days held in audit, plus one week's Medicare billings waiting approval hung up in audit.

For instance:

$37,000 (average daily revenue this month)		
x 3 days	=	$111,000
One week Medicare billings	=	$60,000
Total	=	$171,000

In-house standard

You average 10 days per patient stay. For instance, 10 x average daily revenue. For this month: $37,000 x 10 days = $370,000.

After you and the business office staff have determined days and collection goals, you may want to invite the entire staff to contribute ideas for lowering your receivables and reaching overall goals. Brainstorming sessions are great for generating ideas.

Reports generated from the goal-setting process will provide you with tight control and a good overall picture. These reports also provide your staff with feedback and a sense of achievement, recognition and accomplishment.

Participation in goal setting leads to substantial improvements in performance. You should notice the impact of a well-developed goal setting program in your department within a few months. Goals give focus for the entire staff and make the work considerably more interesting and rewarding for everyone, and more profitable for the hospital.

21
Keep Score

Keeping tabs on the right numbers in receivables will keep senior executives informed on performance and help spot problems before they get out of hand.

STAY INFORMED ON KEY INDICATORS

Keeping tabs on the right numbers in receivables will keep hospital senior executives informed on performance and help spot problems before they get out of hand.

Interestingly enough, hospital CEOs want better reports regarding accounts receivable and collections. Believe it or not, it's the number one item on their wish list of data-based reports ranked by importance (see chart).

In a recent survey of the nation's hospitals, CEOs ranked their desire for better reporting. Surprisingly to us, the condition of receivables and collections came out as their top concern.

If you are a CFO, this means you may want to develop ways

to report the condition of receivables and collection effectiveness to your CEO.

CEO wish list of data-based reports ranked by importance:[1]

Accounts receivable/collections	90.8%
Monthly profit and loss (gross and net revenue)	88.6
Monitoring physician quality	85.1
Employee productivity	82.7
Physician admission patterns	82.1
Departmental utilization	81.6
Payer performance	78.3
Cost accounting (cost per case, product line, physician)	75.8
The effect of physician practice patterns on resources	75.8
Use of hospital resources in relation to patient outcomes	73.7
Comparative data from other hospitals	72.2
Analysis of charges	71.6
Profitability forecasts	66.8
Procedures pricing	61.2
Reports on severity of patient illness	58.2

Recommendation:

Develop a reporting format for the CEO that could look like the following:

[1] *Hospitals* magazine, 1991.

Receivables summary report to CEO

	This month	Last month	YTD
1. Gross days revenue outstanding	____	____	____
2. Net days revenue outstanding	____	____	____
3. Charity write-off	$____	$____	$____
4. Charity write-off; % of gross revenue YTD ...	____	____	____
5. Bad debt write-off	$____	$____	$____
6. Bad debt write-off; % of gross revenue YTD	____	____	____

7. Billing backlogs		Backlog this month	Backlog last month
Total outpatient:	Number	____	____
	Dollars	____	____
Total inpatient:	Number	____	____
	Dollars	____	____
Medical records:	Number	____	____
	Dollars	____	____

		This month	Last month
8. Discharged aging over 90 days	Number	____	____
	Dollars	____	____
	Percent	____	____
9. Total aging over 90 days	Number	____	____
	Dollars	____	____
	Percent	____	____
10. Self-pay in ATB	Number	____	____
	Dollars	____	____
	Percent	____	____
11. Cashier collections	Number	____	____
	Dollars	____	____
12. Collections	Self-pay ...	____	____
	Commercial	____	____
	Blue Cross	____	____
	HMO	____	____
	Medicare ..	____	____
	Medicaid ..	____	____
	Other	____	____
	TOTAL	____	____
13. Inpatient discharge-to-bill time	Medicare ..	____	____
	Other	____	____

STATISTICS CAN LIE

However, if you are a CEO or CFO reading this, numbers can be misleading.

Statistics do lie—at least the statistics we all look at related to hospital accounts receivable.

Days outstanding, bad debt and the aged trial balance are at least three areas that send misleading and mixed signals for a variety of reasons.

Days outstanding:
All national and regional figures are misleading because no one figures them in the same way any more. The most recent HAS/Monitrend II from the American Hospital Association shows hospital net days higher than gross. If all hospitals report net and gross the way they are supposed to be recorded, having net higher than gross is a mathematical impossibility.

Some hospitals adjust receivables to remove all contractual allowances, but leave them in the gross revenue. This makes the gross revenue outstanding figure confusing and the reported days in a mess.

For the first time since the 1986 start-up of the nation's largest hospital receivable survey, the *HARA (Hospital Accounts Receivable Analysis)*, 20 percent of the nation's hospitals are reporting GDRO under 60. Previously, it had been running around 10 percent of the hospitals.

Our 1992 data indicates more and more hospitals (more than 50 percent) are reporting a "gross/net GDRO."

Gross/net phenomenon
Total outstanding receivable
minus contractuals at time of billing
divided by the gross average daily revenue
(not net of contractual)
equals gross days revenue outstanding

Performance indicators that are impacted by accounting changes do not mean improved performance. If your GDRO is down due to a change in the way you report revenue, don't kid yourself into believing you've won the battle to improve your turnaround time.

Everett Veldman, vice president and treasurer at Blodgett Memorial Medical Center, Grand Rapids, Mich., told me he feels hospitals are playing a "numbers game." Veldman told me: "Are hospitals taking contractual discounts from gross patient revenue? If not, it seems to me they are bastardizing the days calculation formula by having the numerator at net and denominator at gross.

"It also seems to me that, arithmetically, a shift from gross to net for **both sides** of the calculation fraction would have no, or nil, impact upon the quotient days. My cynical bet it that there is some game-playing taking place. On the other hand, perhaps I'm just envious of the five-day drop."

In addition, not everyone takes their contractual allowances out of the receivables at the *same time*. Some take them out at time of billing, some within 30 days of discharge, and some hospitals don't take allowances out until the third party insurance pays or the account is paid in full.

Our recent survey showed a 10 percent increase in hospitals that process Medicare contractuals within 30 days of discharge, within the last year. Now, it's about half of the nation's hospitals. This practice is common in hospitals with less than 60 GDRO and tends to reduce days without impacting cash flow. It provides some explanation of the somewhat "cosmetic" reduction in GDRO over the last four quarters. The stats lie.

Bad debt:

The write-off to bad debt tracking is a little less of the "apples to oranges" comparison, but still means different things to different people. Some hospitals record the bad debt as a gross write-off to gross revenue. Others use net write-off *after* recovery from collection agencies, and still others do not officially write off until the agency returns the account as uncollectible.

Aged trial balance:

Our recent national surveys show more than half of the nation's hospitals do not prorate insurance from the patient's portion before the bill is cut—or even before the bill is paid by the insurance. *Therefore, you've probably got ATBs that have wrong numbers in nearly all financial classes.*

Discharged receivables aging over 90 days continue to climb, as the national average represented 31 percent of the A/R. Receivables over 120 days bulged to their highest level since the first quarter of 1989, and are now 22.6 percent of the total ATB. However, equally concerning to the financial manager is the fact half of the hospitals don't really know how much they have in each financial class because they don't prorate.

PURIFY THE NUMBERS FOR THE "TRUTH"

When financial managers are using these three major indicators to measure the value and true condition of their receivables—and the stats are not "*pure*"—an open manhole could lie within the next few steps and the managers wouldn't even know it.

Our suggestion would be to purify your major indicators. Make net *really* net days, keep your write-off as gross and prorate all bills prior to discharge. *Avoid stats that lie.*

The amount of information generated by a growing receivables makes data selection just as important as the information itself.

Generally, when accounts receivable grow and become more complex, the amount of data received by top management also grows. This "information explosion" is also fueled by computerization.

Despite the availability of data, management often lacks the information needed to solve receivables problems. Either the specific information does not exist, or it is lost in the overabundance of data.

An efficient management information system keeps CEOs and CFOs informed both of how the department is presently performing and how it should be performing. The information system also enables RMs to compare data on current performance with past results and future projections.

There are at least five key areas to monitor closely when managing hospital receivables. By tracking the performance in these critical pressure points (listed below), CFOs can stay on top of potential problems that could otherwise go unnoticed for a prolonged period of time.

Left unchecked, poor performance in these five "links in the chain" could spell financial disaster. On the other hand, close control in these areas could produce successful results.

Here are the five particular control points to track and analyze on a regular basis.

KEY PRESSURE POINTS TO MONITOR

1. Preadmission period

Here you would want to track percent of inpatients being preadmitted. The higher the percentage, the greater opportunity you have to investigate and make financial arrangements ahead of time. This also is the time to spot serious collection problems.

In addition to preadmission percentages, other performance indicators would include:

- Percent of admissions with completed insurance verifications.
- Dollar amount of deposits.
- Staff physicians who do and do not cooperate in the preadmission process.

2. Inpatient in-house period

Since the majority of your revenue will come through the inpatient area, you will want to monitor this period closely. Items to track would be:

- Percent of patients in-house with insurance proration showing some kind of report.
- Percent of patients with patient portion over $1,000 without financial arrangements made prior to discharge.
- Total dollars in patient portion for all patients in-house.

3. Inpatient discharge period

Closely connected to a good "up-front" preadmission or in-house monitoring program is a well-organized **discharge system**.

Close control of account balances while patients are hospitalized will help reduce large balance surprises. But, tight control of the payment or arrangements of the patient's portion of the bill *after the service has been rendered* will go a long way toward keeping the self-pay portion of your receivables where you want them.

The discharge interview of the patient or the financially responsible party conducted by the cashier, collector or patient account manager is a critical catch point of increasing collections and reducing self-pay collection problems later on. It will also reduce your bad debt.

Here are some suggested performance indicators to measure and monitor on a timely basis in this financial link:

- Amount of self-pay owed and amount collected at inpatient discharge.
- Number and dollar amount of credit card usage.
- Number and dollar amount of bank notes signed at discharge.
- Percent of discharges that stopped at cashier's area prior to going home.

4. Billing period

Tracking the speed accounts move through this process may be one of the most critical of the five pressure points. Close monitoring would include these areas:

- Number and dollar amount not in a billing mode (broken down by the in-audit stage, or tied up in medical records, late charges, etc.).
- Billing backlogs—by inpatient, outpatient, emergency room, financial class—in each of the above and by biller.

5. Collection period

This covers the entire collection process—both insurance and self-pay. Track and analyze these performance indicators:

- Dollars collected by inpatient, outpatient, by class in both, by collector responsibility.
- Aged trial balance by the same breakout as above.
- Percent of discharged ATB over 90 days.
- Charity and bad debt by inpatient, outpatient and by collector responsibility.

CFOs may want to review these key performance reports at least monthly, and maybe more often in smaller hospitals. The point is to analyze the data frequently enough to take action when the information doesn't look right, or when troublesome trends begin to surface. Tracking the critical areas, analyzing the data regularly and taking the necessary action is the management combination for a faster turnaround of the receivables.

Cash flow in hospitals can change in a hurry. Or so it seems.

However, deteriorating accounts receivable doesn't happen overnight. It slowly begins to erode until your cash flow suddenly becomes affected.

There are several key telltale signs that can alert you to potential problems in receivables. If you spot them in time and act quickly to correct the causes of the problems, you may avoid a cash-flow squeeze.

Here are some signs to detect receivable problems that will eventually affect cash flow:

10 SIGNS OF PROBLEMS

1. An increase of dollars in accounts receivable outstanding of more than 10 percent over one year ago (even if you've had a rate increase or occupancy jump)—Is a signal to review.
2. An increase in the number of open accounts compared to a year ago. Any increase needs a closer look.
3. An increase in bad debt of ½ of 1 percent over one year ago.
4. Bad debt over 5 percent of gross charges.
5. An increase in medical record delays. Any time your total dollars in receivables delayed in medical records exceeds 10 percent of total receivables—or over 5 days in days revenue outstanding—it spells trouble.
6. An increase in percent of receivables over 90 days. Any percentage over 22 in total receivables over 90 days means cash is turning too slowly.
7. Increases in self-pay or commercial insurance financial classes of your accounts receivable. These are your most "profitable" financial classes. Any increase in total dollars in

these two financial classes could spell real financial disaster in operating profit and cash flow in the near future.

8. An increase in net days revenue outstanding over 5 days from one year ago, and anytime you exceed 80 net days revenue outstanding, means your financial picture and cash flow is deteriorating.
9. Cash collections not keeping up with, or exceeding, net amount billed each month. If your collections start to fall behind or just keep up with net dollars billed, you could begin to see cash flow problems.
10. If total cash collections begin to dip under 96 percent of net revenue for four consecutive months:

TIP:

a. Track these vital receivables stats on a monthly basis.

b. Investigate early signs of a problem. Determine the cause.

c. Act on solutions. Don't procrastinate.

22

Hold Receivables Manager Accountable

If you're keeping score, you should be able to hold key people accountable for the results.

ACCOUNTABLE FOR RESULTS

If you're keeping score, you should be able to hold the people accountable for the results.

Where's the beef? Remember the TV commercial? It was one fast-food chain giving one of its competitors a zinger. But if receivables lie in your area of responsibility, how about this one—"Where's the accountability?"

When you look at any particular aspect of the receivables management process as a senior executive, do you find yourself asking, "Who is responsible (accountable is a better, more appropriate word) for this?" When people "feel accountable" and are "held accountable," you probably won't have a "beef" to complain about. Holding people accountable for results is a must.

The person who must to be held accountable for the condition of receivables is the manger of that department. If you're not going to hold the receivables manager accountable for results in this area, why did you hire that person in the first place?

Of course, the CFO must accept the ultimate responsibility for the overall financial condition of the hospital. So does the CEO these days. In truth, it's a shared responsibility. But the manager of receivables must be accountable for the receivables results.

CEOs AND CFOs FIND THIS DIFFICULT

Many hospital CEOs and CFOs I have met in the past 25 years dance around with this "hold them accountable" idea when it comes to receivables managers. Senior hospital executives find it extremely difficult, if not impossible, to fire incompetent receivable managers. They make excuses for them, dodge the pink-slip bullet and just won't pull the trigger, even though the incompetency is costing the hospital good cash flow and perhaps millions in profit.

When receivables managers are not held accountable for results, they become even more complacent. I've seen it happen time and again. In fact, I've seen it cost a CFO his job because he couldn't get rid of the non-performing manager. The CFO was gone, and the lousy receivables manager that cost the CFO his job was still there.

For instance, isn't it rather ironic that while hospitals are experiencing serious financial problems, managers in charge of receivables "feel completely secure" in their position?

A recent national survey of hospital receivables managers showed that 90 percent said they "felt secure" in their position at the present time. Why on earth is that? Is it because, no matter how bad things get for the hospital financially, these managers don't feel responsible? Or is it because their CFOs don't hold them more accountable for results? Or have they become complacent?

It could be as simple as these managers not understanding the importance of their role in the financial health of the hospital—and, no matter what happens, they're "safe."

It might be advisable to review goals and establish accountability with the managers of receivables so that, in their mind, *security is synonymous with results.*

You may think a good work ethic is a foreign concept. Your staff may not be working as hard or long as they should. Although "face time" (showing up at work but not necessarily doing anything worthwhile) and image have replaced honest effort on many employees' priority lists, they still feel entitled to their jobs, benefits and paychecks.

MEDIOCRITY CAN BECOME THE NORM

You share responsibility for this dilemma by failing to hold people accountable for doing good work. Worse, CFOs who tolerate mediocrity and evaluate performance half-heartedly promote a blinding group-think mentality: Once mediocrity becomes the norm, workers believe they're making progress when in fact they're standing still.

Psychological research confirms that motivation is highest when the odds of success are fifty-fifty. People don't really get excited about jobs that are too easy or too hard. To create a winning psychology, you must move people to a middle range of risk while consistently supporting their efforts. The goal isn't to create fear, but rather to create anxiety high enough to stimulate achievement. Here are some ways to guide your people toward accountability:[1]

1. **Identify and evaluate "real work."** To increase pressure, you must first identify what constitutes real work (don't confuse activity with achievement).

   Identifying real work naturally leads to evaluating real performance. One good way to do this is to use measurable targets. Create opportunities for challenge and risk-taking by releasing people for special assignments and job rotation. Each year, 25 percent of a person's job should be new.
2. **Increase visibility and peer pressure.** Leaner, flatter departments offer fewer niches where people can hide. Assign work to small groups of people of similar status whenever possible. By evaluating group instead of individual performance you increase group bonding and emotional support, and encourage peer pressure. People will feel responsible for achieving, not only because they'll be held accountable, but also because they realize the group won't tolerate goof-offs.
3. **Consider incentive pay plans.** Incentive pay plans also tend to hone performance to a keen edge. They promote a winning psychology simply because people get too apathetic when none of their pay is at risk. Some 75 percent of American employers have at least one kind of incentive pay plan today.

   Incentive pay isn't just for RMs, however. It should apply to everyone—billers, collectors and registrars.
4. **Fire for nonperformance.** If firing becomes necessary, leave no doubt that those you discharged were underachievers who received ample evaluation, guidance and support to help them perform at an acceptable level. Make certain everyone knows that firing is an option.

The work ethic may be better than you think.

[1] Judith M. Bardwick, *Danger in the Comfort Zone.*

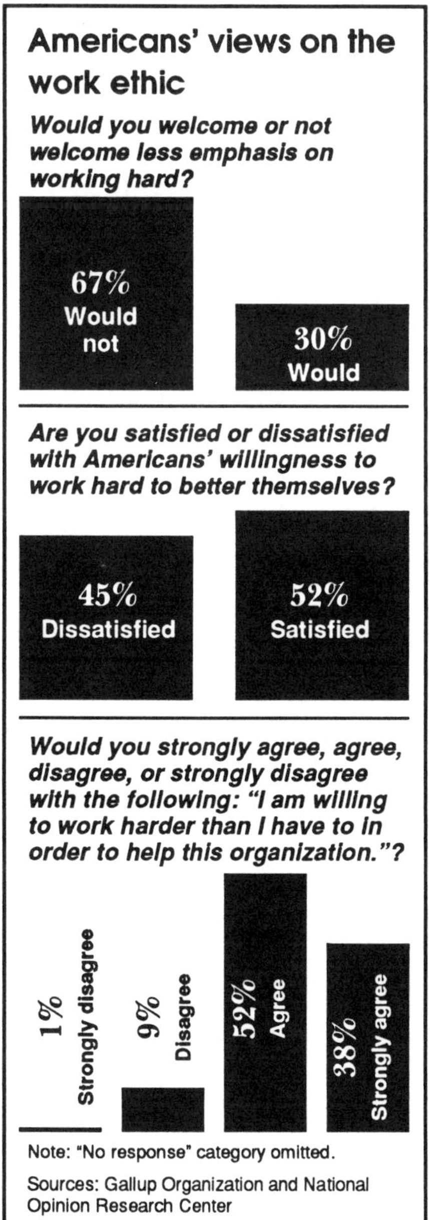

A recent survey by the Gallup Poll and the National Opinion Research Center shows your employees are willing to work harder. The trick is to use good motivational skills and to hire the right people.

According to Tom Peters, 14 percent of the workforce in the USA "doesn't care." He then adds, "But you don't have to hire them."

Some companies are using psychological assessments of job applicants to weed out the 14 percent who don't care. After all, conventional interviews don't always uncover an applicant's real attitude towards work.

While this added step in the interviewing process is expensive and time consuming, it may be worth it. Turnover is also expensive—or even worse, you can get "stuck" with unproductive employees.

Not holding managers accountable and not firing for nonperformance is looking at accountability from the negative side. Let's face it, no one likes to fire someone. But everyone likes to see their employees succeed.

Letting managers know you're holding them accountable is actually motivating and helps them succeed. Most employees worth keeping on staff respond favorably to being counted on to produce. It helps them feel needed and increases their self-esteem. Those who don't respond favorably shouldn't work at your hospital anyway.

23

TQM and Cash

Total Quality Management concepts can work in improving cash flow

TQM IS HOT

Total Quality Management is hot in hospitals and it can tie in to improving cash flow.

Deloitte & Touche recently pointed out that more and more hospitals are now using some kind of TQM or CQI (Continuous Quality Improvement).

Currently, nearly 60 percent of U.S. hospitals have a TQM/Continuous Quality Improvement program in place, according to a March survey conducted by *Hospitals* magazine. The survey points out that, three years ago, 15 percent of all hospitals were using some kind of CQI.

There has been a tremendous increase in the interest of hospitals in quality management in terms of formal programs.

The trend is that hospitals will continue to look at these formal quality improvement programs. Surveys indicate doctors are buying into TQM and CQI.

What is the potential impact of Continuous Quality Improvement on hospital cash flow? At least one CFO believes it can make a real difference.

"We have seen our receivables drop, cash (flow) improve and patient complaints decline," says Dave Albrecht, vice president of finance at Bellin Memorial Hospital in Green Bay, Wis. He explained that, although the hospital has been involved in a quality improvement program for almost two years, it was actively implemented in the business office only recently.

"The results have been impressive, and are probably even more significant because the entire financial team, from controller to insurance billers, was actively involved in the process," Albrecht said. "Employees are excited about our accomplishments, and we have a good time setting our objectives and celebrating our progress. Our commitment to ongoing quality improvement requires that the team evaluate itself by the total quality of the product we supply our internal and external customers."

"Too often in the past, we were satisfied if most of our departments met budget objectives, or other department-specific goals were attained," Albrecht said. "We spent a lot of time assessing blame and finding fault in other operations. CQI is customer-focused and quality driven. The process relies on each member of an organization building quality into all aspects of service development and delivery. We are only successful if the organization meets its stated mission, and our customers—patients, physicians, other hospital departments—are delighted with our product. The objective is to exceed expectations, not just meet them."

JCAHO ALSO CONVINCED

The Joint Commission on Accreditation of Health Care Organizations also appears to be convinced. New standards, which will be published in the 1992 edition of the JCAHO's Accreditation Manual for Hospitals, will require all hospital CEOs to educate themselves on CQI methods. We believe the adoption of these standards signals a new, serious concern on the part of the commission regarding hospital commitment to quality management.

Evidence from non-health care industries supports the position that improved quality is good for business. A survey of 351 quality assurance professionals, conducted by the American Society for Quality Control, shows that only 2 percent of respondents were "frustrated" with the results of their quality efforts. The government's General Accounting Office also found that companies adopting TQM practices "experienced an overall improvement in corporate performance," and that the concept is effective in both small and large facilities.

One of the basic tenets of the classic Deming quality model is the elimination of fear associated with taking responsibility for one's actions. As a result, he suggests the elimination of the management by objectives philosophy. In too many organizations, the process of objective-setting has become a top-down process of intimidation. The original idea, as advocated by Peter Drucker in his book, *The Practice of Management,* was that employees would be motivated if they set their own objectives. Unfortunately, in some institutions, the MBO process became distorted and bureaucraticized into a system of top-down control.

However, CQI requires score keeping for both quality measures and business measures. Score keeping requires setting objectives. The key is that the most useful objectives are set by those who must perform.

If you want to implement CQI, we suggest you thoroughly understand the underlying philosophy of quality improvement as well as the specific tools, techniques and approaches that can be used to achieve it. Get a "buy in" from all levels of management, and a commitment from the hospital board of directors.

Because it's "hot," many hospitals will begin to address the specifics of CQI implementation by devising a short-term strategic plan that maps out the first year or two of development, establishing basic process and resource allocations. Logistics and organization-wide communication must be well coordinated.

WRONG FOCUS CAN HURT DESIRED RESULTS

Measuring productivity is good. Focusing on only one aspect of production is bad. We have found a surprising number of hospital financial executives focusing in on information which actually *hampers* productivity.

This problem is heightened over the past few years due to rising employee costs and the new competitive nature of our industry. Ten years ago, an FTE in the business office cost you $14,756 (including benefits). Today, that same person will cost you $20,011. (This is a modest calculation, based on a 3 percent annual increase.) We all agree that, unless each employee is productive, we cannot justify his or her salary and benefits. Most of us would further agree that, if we are in doubt as to a worker's productivity level of capability, the worker has a strong chance of being terminated.

Management's full-time employee "productivity logic" has evolved during the past few years into an employee's nightmare. Instead of increasing the ranks as we try to assume more of the collection responsibility in-house, most hospital managers have concentrated on downsizing, streamlining and becoming lean health care machines.

Managers are measuring the total number of accounts registered, billed, contacted, etc., and are ignoring the number of incomplete registrations, rebills and insufficient collection follow-up. By creating a system of checks and balances to justify our workers, managers often have indirectly shifted workers' priorities, and are awarding an "incomplete" job. *It too often becomes quantity over quality.*

Although we might not want to recognize this error, we have created an environment which *promotes quantity* handled and *ignores quality.* An insufficient job may take up to six months to be found and corrected. This pushes payment further away. Quality does impact payment.

You may want to take a look at your department's employee tracking system and prioritize a job done *correctly.* Give *quality of work* equal billing. Quality pays.

TIPS TO CONQUER QUALITY ISSUES

1. Audit returned or delayed insurance billing to determine if quality of information or billing created a problem. Track and analyze audit information. Do this on a routine basis, not just once in awhile. The quality problems may lie in the admission process or in the billing unit. But, you'll know specifics. Act on the findings.
2. Audit accounts written off to bad debt to determine quality of collection effort and effectiveness. Track and analyze information periodically. Act on the findings. Your collectors may need more training. You may need more collectors, or you may need different collectors.

3. Audit inpatient discharge process. What's the quality of payment on the patient's portion? Track what should have been paid vs. what was paid. If you don't collect self-pay at discharge, your risk of never collecting increases dramatically. Track and analyze findings on a routine basis. This is probably one of your biggest holes in the entire self-pay collection process.

24

Deal with Medical Record Delays

Too much of hospital receivables tied up in medical records, but CEOs and CFOs treat problem like hot potato.

MEDICAL RECORDS DELAYS HOT POTATO

Too much of your receivables is probably tied up in medical records. Because it deals with the medical staff, many CEOs and CFOs treat this problem like a hot potato. They don't want to deal with it.

What would you do for an additional $1.7 billion in collections? Nationally, that is the amount of hospital accounts receivable delayed due to incomplete medical records.

According to *HARA*[1], 9 percent of total accounts receivable are tied up in medical records. That would buy a $2 million CAT scan for a few hospitals in the country.

With pressure on hospital CFOs to turn around their

[1] Zimmerman & Associates, Inc., *HARA (Hospital Accounts Receivable Analysis)*, 1992.

accounts receivable, medical record delays have become a big concern. Because of relationships between physician and hospital, this subject has often only received lip service.

Hospitals have come up with some very creative ideas to entice their medical staff members to complete their records. Remember, however, this area is also closely looked at by Healthcare Financing Administration, so do not make it appear that you are "buying" the physicians' admissions.

Some hospitals have taken a very conservative approach and sponsored luncheons, pizza parties or provided food for medical staff members when they complete their records. Others provide office support, billing information, etc. to staff members for staying current with their charts.

CREATIVITY SCORES

With a little more creativity, you will find the hospitals that made a game out of the process were more successful. For instance, awarding a pen set to the physician who has signed attestations.

One hospital had a putting green in the physicians lounge and they scored points toward gifts based on their putting accuracy. Their incomplete medical records determined the distance of their putt.

Some hospitals simply held contests and rewarded prizes to the physician with the best/shortest time period for completing medical records. Prizes ranged from cash, gift certificates to restaurants or the theater, and once, going as far as a free trip to Mexico.

Usually, the more severe a problem in delayed medical records, the greater the inducement.

What does all this mean?

You need to develop a program or mechanism to ensure your

medical staff realizes the financial impact they have on your institution. And, based upon the interests of your medical staff and creativity of your medical records director, you can do almost anything.

One hospital tried a unique approach to dealing with this dilemma. The Community Hospital in Munster, Ind., has taken steps to reduce their medical records delay and at the same time improve relations with the medical staff.

According to Susan Adams, patient accounts manager, the hospital has initiated a program of providing the medical staff with a signed "Assignment of Benefits" for physician bills and complete billing information. This information is obtained after the hospital has verified the patient's insurance coverage.

This information will provide physician's office staff members with everything they will need to properly bill the patient's insurance and receive payment directly from the insurance company, thereby reducing the physician's outstanding accounts receivable.

This service is provided to all attending and consulting staff physicians who have kept delinquent medical records to a minimum (set by the hospital).

Simply put, the hospital feels if physicians are concerned enough to allow the hospital to bill for their services, they will provide any assistance they can to allow the physician to bill for the hospital's services.

This proven method may be one that can be implemented at your hospital.

Everyone is interested in reducing medical record delays. But how many hospitals are committed? Chances are, not enough. For example, *HARA (Hospital Accounts Receivable Analysis)* shows nearly 60 percent of all medical record departments do not report to the finance department.

In my experience, commitment to medical record improvement is more difficult when medical records reports to operations, or nursing. Although it does not automatically follow that switching medical records to finance magically reduces delays, a good understanding of financial resources tied up in medical records gets better results.

MEDICAL RECORDS DOES NOT REPORT TO FINANCE

So, what can you do if medical records does not report to your area? Here are some suggestions:

1. Publish medical record delays on a weekly basis. Let everyone know the financial impact.
2. Gain a commitment for reduction of record delays. Report on goal to actual activity on a weekly basis.
3. Work together with medical records management. Go to bat for them. If additional resources are needed to reduce medical record delays, do what you can to help out.
4. Don't give up, or accept the status quo. If medical record delays are negatively impacting **your** days, let the world know about it. Don't accept mediocrity in this area.

With Medicare making up the largest piece of your payer mix, it is more important now than ever that your claims go out the door quickly and correctly. Medical records, doctors, nurses, admissions, registration, and credit and verification all need to pull together and work as a team so these delays don't severely disrupt your cash flow.

More attention should be paid to correct coding and thorough documentation being sent with the claim, instead of waiting for Medicare to reject for lack of supporting documentation. Charge Data Masters should be kept up to date and with the most current coding to effect the maximum DRG reimbursement amounts.

Claim rejection vouchers should be worked immediately to minimize any further delays in payment. Tracking and analysis of rejections are also imperative so repeated errors do not occur.

Create a sense of urgency in completing medical records. Administration must be kept informed. Reinforce the delinquency policy to those physicians not meeting requirements.

Medical records staff should be assigned to monitor and assist primary physicians. Keep physicians informed of their backlogs. Ensure records are available when physicians have scheduled time for this process.

Data processing should provide support in chart tracking and assembly to supply the tools needed to track and monitor all deficient records.

Administration and the medical staff need reports to identify by physician the number, age and dollars associated with incomplete records. Records need to be located where more physicians can have access to the charts.

In short, set up an aggressive program to combat medical record delays. Despite all you may have done, you've probably still got far too much cash tied up here. Involve hospital boards, physicians and the medical records department.

25

Benchmarking: Measuring Yourself Against the Best

Want to get better fast? Learn from the hospitals who do it best.

SOME HOSPITALS IN FAVORABLE POSITION

Want to get better fast? Learn from the hospitals who do it best.

Desperate times breed desperate actions. Some hospitals have decided to take dramatically different approaches to managing receivables, and thereby put themselves in a much more favorable financial situation.

Turning around financially-troubled hospitals will take on a new meaning in the '90s. It will become the central theme for hospitals. There are some who have gotten a head start. Consider the following we have come across just for starters.

A 560-bed hospital in Fort Worth, Texas, reduces its days revenue outstanding by 46, going from 104 to 58, and increases reserves by over $5 million; in highly-regulated Massachusetts, a 350-bed hospital drops from 110 to 63 days, and offsets a serious cash flow problem in the process; a 545-bed hospital in Florida, losing $3.5 million a year, reduces days outstanding from 114 to 46 and begins to make a profit for the first time in years; a 456-bed institution in Michigan reduces receivables by $20 million, days by 62 and creates a $39 million swing; a southern California hospital with 363 beds produces a 55-day reduction in days outstanding, going from 102 to 47 and adds over $5 million to reserves in the process!

SOUNDER FINANCIAL FOOTINGS

All of these actual turnarounds took less than three years. All are on much sounder financial footing since they started their turnaround program. And it was accomplished primarily by better management of their receivables.

So, some hospitals have already begun their receivables turnaround. There are more than a few hospitals in the nation that have taken themselves from serious cash flow problems to financial success in a relatively short time.

These hospital financial managers may not have known the proper term when I interviewed them, but when they started their turnaround, it was a benchmarking project. They each told me—*they wanted to be among the best.*

Benchmarking is a process of finding the world-class examples of a product, service or operational system, and then adjusting your products, services or systems to meet or beat that standard. The term, originally used by land surveyors to compare elevations, was pioneered in the U.S. business world by Xerox Corporation in the late 1970s.

Benchmarking can be a foundation of any receivables improvement program. If a hospital wants to be the best, it must know how the current stars manage to be so good. And it must then measure itself against those standards.

Our advice—first, decide you need to improve, then hunt for the hospitals that do their best!

Here are some composite statistics of some of the best performing hospitals in the nation.[2]

Check your figures against some of the best.[3]

	U.S. average	The best	The worst
Bad debt[2]	3.8%	2.9%	6.2%
Charity	2.1%	1.1%	2.7%
Total uncollectible[2]	5.9%	4%	8.9%
Percent of discharged receivables over 90 days	30.5%	23.8%	58%
Average days from discharge-to-bill	12.2	10.7	17
Open accounts per FTE collector	4,100	3,900	5,100
Gross days outstanding	73	54	110

HOW XEROX DOES BENCHMARKING

With its years of experience in benchmarking, Xerox has developed a 10-step model that is used by all departments that want to do benchmarking studies. The steps:

1. **Identify what is to be benchmarked.** It could be something tangible, such as days, bad debt, billing time, or it could be something as intangible as patient satisfaction.
2. **Identify comparative hospitals.** Those are just three simple words, but expect to spend some time on the research.

[2] Percent of gross revenue.

[3] Zimmerman & Associates, Inc., *HARA (Hospital Accounts Receivable Analysis)*, Second Quarter, 1992.

3. **Determine data collection method and collect data.** The teams that conduct the studies determine what measurements will be used.
4. **Determine current performance levels.** Take the measurements of your own function and compare them with the measurements from the benchmarked hospital. That usually produces a negative or positive performance gap. (Sometimes, you'll be pleasantly surprised to find you're better than you thought.)
5. **Project future performance levels.** Use the measurements of the gap to figure out what the new performance goals should be if that gap is to be closed and how long it will take.
6. **Communicate benchmarking findings and gain acceptance.** Present findings and recommendations to higher management for endorsement. Then, they are communicated to employees.
7. **Establish functional goals.** Here's where you write objectives.
8. **Develop action plans.** What good is an objective without a specific plan to achieve it?
9. **Implement the plans and monitor progress.** If the goals aren't being met, problem-solving teams might be formed to figure out why.
10. **Recalibrate measurements.** Are the hospitals you examined still the barometers of excellence? If not, find others and set new goals.

26

Now—What Do You Do with the Cash?

"Please, give me such a problem!"
Hospital CFO

IMPROVEMENT PROVIDES MORE CASH

Hospitals that reduce the days of revenue outstanding and reduce bad debt also end up with more available cash. The same will be true of your hospital as soon as you focus on receivables. Now, what do you do with the cash?

One CFO told me when I asked what he would do with a surplus of cash, "Please, give me such a problem!"

How much actual cash can you generate from an ambitious thrust to lower receivables? The average hospital's daily gross revenue amounts to $340,000. Hospitals are reporting an average of 77 gross days of revenue outstanding. This means, on average, that every day of revenue a hospital can reduce through collection on their A/R will produce upwards of $240,000 of actual cash (after allowances).

However, without an organized cash management plan you may not reap the full benefits of an infusion of cash. A cash management plan or profile should outline your requirements tied to operating and capital budgets. A detailed plan would cover how and when your surplus cash should be used and handled.

Some CFOs we spoke with have shared their thoughts on their operations and cash management plans after they experienced a turnaround in their receivables.

- **Brought in outside money manager:**
  A CFO of a small Chicago-area hospital stated all their excess cash was directed for investment by their finance committee. They brought in an outside money manager to handle the majority of their funds because, in his words, "I couldn't hire anyone to handle this job for the fees I am paying."

  The CFO also handles some short-term funds directly invested in high-grade commercial paper.
- **Rely on CFO:**
  A large hospital in Florida chose to rely solely on the CFO. Their finance committee directs the amount of funds to be invested, all of which is placed in short-term securities. The CFO stated the hospital has established a precedent of an extremely conservative approach utilizing only U.S. Government Securities.
- **Short-term CDs in local bank:**
  In Kansas, a 400-bed medical center maintains their funds in short-term CDs at local banks. Their controller stated it's more of a political move, or a means of support, for their local community. They may forego a few basis points, but feel it's worth it.

Investment returns from 1926 - 1989[1]			
	Nominal returns (includes inflation)	Real returns (excludes inflation)	Real growth of $1
U.S. Treasury bills	3.6%	.5%	$ 1.37
Long-term government bonds	4.6%	1.4%	$ 2.46
U.S. stocks	10.3%	7.0%	$75.98

- **Used cash for vendor discounts**

  The CFO of a Midwestern metropolitan medical center was not as quick as others to invest excess cash. He felt they could receive maximum benefits by re-negotiating all vendors and supply contracts.

  With the available cash, he could take advantage of creative discount programs and ultimately reduce operating expenses. As an added benefit, all daily cash was placed in a cash management fund provided by their banking facility. This allowed interest earnings on all cash from day one, regardless of its final destination.

Depending on the goals of your institution, funds are utilized in various avenues. You may feel local investments support the community, or you may place your investments with a facility that has always financially supported the hospital.

However, this route may not always provide the highest return. Try and quantify the value of your investments. Are you receiving the best return, whether it be in dollars or some other asset?

GET PROFESSIONAL MONEY MANAGER

With the current state of our financial markets, who can say what investments are safe, or which provide the best returns? It appears that most health care financial managers feel, to

[1] Hewitt Associates

receive optimum returns, you need to engage the services of a professional money manager.

The selection of a financial manager can be a monumental task in itself. In addition to the limitless number of financial brokers, there are those specifically available to hospitals. Many state hospital associations have pooled programs for hospitals. The Hospital Fund Inc. of New Haven, Conn., a non-profit fund, invests exclusively for the health care industry. All can provide avenues to handle your investments.

In choosing an outside manager, look at past performance and at future projections, and examine his/her investment portfolio. Does it provide the level of safety or risk you are looking for? Check current and past clients. Is the manager able to serve your account, and provide the expertise you will need?

Stock performance in bear markets since 1929

Year started	Decline (in percent)	Length (in months)
1929	89	34
1934	23	6
1937	49	13
1938	41	42
1946	24	37
1961	27	6
1966	25	8
1968	36	18
1973	45	23
1976	27	17
1981	24	15
1987	36	2

Source: Charles Will Investments Inc., Stovall/Twenty-first Consistent Return Trust

After you have selected a manager, track and monitor results. Compare against comparable benchmarks and results of other managers.

Robert Moseson, president of Performance Analytics Inc., a Chicago-based consulting firm, suggests that you allow managers three years to perform well. If after this period, you do not get results and they perform in the lower half of their peer group comparisons, give them a period of one year to improve. If they don't, remove them.

HERE'S WHAT YOU CAN DO

- Decide who will invest what amounts of your cash.
- If you choose to use a money manager, make selection based upon proven track record.
- Check on past and current client references.
- Allow a period of up to three years to fully evaluate performance.
- Track their results and compare to other managers and key indicators.
- If investments are placed for specific strategic reasons or political reasons, quantify the results to make valid comparisons on performance.
- Investigate other benefits that can be achieved with your cash on hand—new purchasing contracts, etc.
- Measure and track the benefits of such purchasing contracts.

What to do with the cash? I'm sure that won't be a problem for you. That's the reason this is the book's shortest chapter.

27

The Best Years of Your Life

Senior executives have, at this time and place in history, the opportunity to lead the industry in the right direction.

TIME TO THINK

As I finish the final chapter of this book, I'm sitting at a kitchen table in a small cottage in a heavily wooded area of northern Wisconsin. I've been alone here for nearly a week, pushing hard to wrap up this project I started nearly two years ago.

It's autumn here now. The foliage at this time of year in this part of the country is simply breathtaking. Mother Nature mixes and matches all her pigments to produce the tones and shades that give color to the brilliantly radiant landscape.

When you're completely alone in this kind of surrounding, you have more time to think and contemplate. I know I have. For instance, I've been reflecting on how fortunate I am to have a wonderful (and blessed with a large) family (10 children), and a loving wife, good health, a great job, competent and enthusiastic associates in my firm, and some valued friendships.

I'm thinking, these are probably the best years of my life.

But, as I bring this project to a close, it also occurs to me that, as a hospital executive, these could also be the best years of your life. Right now.

Why would I say that knowing the tremendous difficulties most of you are struggling with in today's entangled hospital environment?

Because, it seems to me, that our industry is at some kind of crossroad. We can go to the left or right. Either we go to the left and improve internal management, enhance the delivery and reimbursement system in health care, thereby curtailing increasing costs—or the industry stumbles its way along on the road to the right and into the devouring arms of the liberals and government, where cataclysmic control, regulation and stagnation will result in inferior health care. Our world-class medical practice would become second-rate.

LEAD THE INDUSTRY

As senior executives in health care, you now—at this time and place in history—have the power to lead the industry down either road. Our surveys show very few of you want to turn your career over to the government. That's not the road of your choice.

However, to take the other road perhaps presents the greatest challenge you professionally, or the health care industry, have every faced. That's the key.

This time and place presents an immense challenge—a mountain to climb—a noble undertaking—a chance to literally alter the course of history in our great country where our medical miracles are every day occurrences.

Those of you in your positions have the rare treat and opportunity in today's too often downcast society, to champion a cause. To be in a position to defy the odds and impact the way health care will be administered in the future, is indeed a lofty responsibility.

For those of you who want challenges that impact mankind in a way few others can today, then these are indeed the best years of your life. The best time to be able to contribute—to be needed.

Regardless of your chronological age, these next few years will provide you with the wonderful opportunity to determine how health care will be delivered in this country in the long years to come. You have the chance to be the *heroes of health care,* so to speak.

The time for self-pity parties is over. Blaming the government or other outside forces for the industry's woes waste time and energy.

The real challenge is to fix it yourselves. Controlling your expenses, hospital costs; improving quality of care, cash flow and profit. These are only a small fraction of the items on your full agenda to fix over the next few years.

But, as we said when we opened the book—*without cash there can be no mission.*

So, whereas improving cash flow and profit from receivables may be only a small percentage of the solution to the problems facing you today, it's certainly an important percent.

It's our belief improved management of receivables can take you a good deal further than you even imagine right now. It's my wish that you take me up on this premise and find out for yourself.

Focusing on cash does not mean the mission is less

important. It just means it is the first priority to be sure the mission can be kept.

Because...cash is king.